The Cognitive Classroom

Using Brain and Cognitive Science to Optimize Student Success

Jerome L. Rekart

ROWMAN & LITTLEFIELD EDUCATION
A division of
ROWMAN & LITTLEFIELD PUBLISHERS, INC.
Lanham • New York • Toronto • Plymouth, UK

Published by Rowman & Littlefield Education
A division of Rowman & Littlefield Publishers, Inc.
A wholly owned subsidiary of The Rowman & Littlefield Publishing Group, Inc.
4501 Forbes Boulevard, Suite 200, Lanham, Maryland 20706
www.rowman.com

10 Thornbury Road, Plymouth PL6 7PP, United Kingdom

Copyright © 2013 by Jerome L. Rekart

All rights reserved. No part of this book may be reproduced in any form or by any electronic or mechanical means, including information storage and retrieval systems, without written permission from the publisher, except by a reviewer who may quote passages in a review.

British Library Cataloguing in Publication Information Available

Library of Congress Cataloging-in-Publication Data

Rekart, Jerome L.
 The cognitive classroom : using brain and cognitive science to optimize student success / Jerome L. Rekart.
  pages cm
 Includes bibliographical references.
 ISBN 978-1-4758-0071-5 (cloth : alk. paper) -- ISBN 978-1-4758-0072-2 (pbk. : alk. paper) -- ISBN 978-1-4758-0073-9 (electronic)
 1. Learning, Psychology of. 2. Cognitive learning theory. 3. Cognition in children. 4. Educational psychology. I. Title.
 LB1060.R445 2013
 370.15'23--dc23
                        2013015538

∞™ The paper used in this publication meets the minimum requirements of American National Standard for Information Sciences Permanence of Paper for Printed Library Materials, ANSI/NISO Z39.48-1992.

Printed in the United States of America

For Sophie, Lucy, and Julie:

may your lives bring you as much wisdom, light,
and beauty as you have brought me

Contents

Preface vii
Introduction xi

1 The Brain and Behavior 1
2 Perception 17
3 Attention 35
4 Working Memory 55
5 Long-term Memory Encoding 71
6 Long-term Memory Retrieval 91
7 Language 109
8 Decision Making 127
9 Problem Solving 141
10 Synthesis 155

Preface

WHY IS THIS BOOK NECESSARY?

Today's educational climate is marked by decreases in the amount of time devoted to teaching non-assessed subjects, such as social studies, the ever-present struggle between teaching for long-term retention and teaching "to the test" (i.e., standardized achievement tests), and a virtual alphabet soup of laws and regulations, initiatives, and assessments, such as NCLB, PBIS, RTI, and NAEP (Ravitch, 2010).

Indeed, the well-*intentioned* but poorly implemented set of educational mandates collectively known as No Child Left Behind (NCLB) has largely failed to bridge the gap between white and minority student achievement and has not produced statistically significant or meaningful gains on national assessments of reading ability—which, ironically, was one impetus behind President George W. Bush's desire to shepherd and sign the largely bipartisan legislation in the first place.

What is particularly striking about all of this is that it is taking place at a time when differentiated instruction and individualized attention for learners has become de rigueur and can not be considered just another educational fad, soon to be replaced by the next newest and best thing.

Indeed, in my conversations with educators, regardless of the particular grade or subject taught, one common theme has emerged. That theme is one that speaks to the tension felt by novice and experienced teachers as well as school administrators. Namely, what is experienced on a daily basis is a tension between the desire to successfully reach all students in a classroom and the need to successfully move the class as a whole through a curriculum.

Though certainly this tension has always been present for the best teachers, it is now amplified greatly by the manner in which student success and achievement are assessed on a yearly basis. If the "stakes" associated with the outcomes of the assessments weren't so high, the stress would be less. Meeting adequate yearly progress (AYP), the government's label for successfully ensuring that no child is left "behind" (though I've often wondered, "behind what or whom?") is an important distinction; failing to do so (i.e., being a "school in need of improvement") results in an incredibly stressful situation with real consequences (e.g., school funding, teacher and administrator jobs).

Despite recent "allowances" by current U.S. Secretary of Education Arne Duncan to loosen the "bite" of these consequences, the era of assessment-driven education and school accountability is likely here to stay. The question remains how does one achieve the balance between attention to individualized learning needs and the needs of the group to achieve a particular level of success?

Adding to the challenges of teaching in America today is the increased diversity of the student population. Changing demographics, including increases in the number of learners for whom English is a second language, contribute to these challenges. There are many benefits to having a more culturally pluralistic society, especially in an ever-"flattening" world (Friedman, 2005).

Students benefit from exposure to new perspectives and to practices that may seem alien. Besides natural barriers imposed by a lack of fluency in a particular language, research now firmly indicates that the beliefs, perspectives, and languages of a culture all can contribute to differences in the ways that individuals actually learn, thus further adding to the complexities of guiding individual learners in a classroom toward a common goal.

Furthermore, though technology may be seen by some as the panacea, the silver bullet, for educational problems, we must take a more nuanced view of the role that technology plays in today's society. Though computers certainly can be a powerful instructional tool, technology not only assists learning but can prove to be an impediment as well (see chapter 3). For example, research suggests that technology is actually changing the way people think and interact with the world around them. These changes may not be readily understood by educators from a different generation, for whom family dinners didn't consist of nightly competitions for attention among face-to-face conversations, text messages, and status updates.

So how is an educator, confronted by the hydra of challenges due to assessment-driven curriculum, changing population demographics, and technological advances able to guide individuals toward common grade-level equivalency? Teaching and learning are psychological phenomena. Indeed all of the mental processes necessary for true, deep learning may be lumped together under the psychological term of *cognition*.

Though not usually classified in this manner, one can easily make the assertion that educators are actually cognitive scientists in their own right; or, if one prefers to be more avant-garde, "practitioners of the cognitive arts." Regardless of the label used, there is no denying the fact that teachers are affecting, employing, and assessing cognition on a near continual basis as a normal course of their daily duties.

Both teaching and learning involve an observable set of behaviors influenced by a number of factors. Learning researchers, those individuals usually referred to as cognitive scientists, have examined many of these factors to determine what affects learning and how. Despite decades of work, for reasons not readily apparent or understood, many of these cognitive scientific findings languish in research journals, unbeknownst to the educators whom could benefit from them the most.

This book looks to move those findings into the forefront of pedagogy. With an emphasis on how most, if not all, *humans* learn, it has been crafted to bridge the divide between education and the learning sciences of cognitive psychology and neuroscience. In the pages and chapters that follow, numerous research findings of direct use to teachers and administrators will be identified and ideas for their implementation in actual K–12 settings will be described. Some of these findings challenge long-held beliefs while others support the efficacy of decades-old "best practices."

This is a book that will help educators achieve replicable and reliable enhancements in the memory and understanding of their students.

Introduction

BASICS OF COGNITION

Teachers facilitate student learning, which only occurs when a memory is created. A memory is a skill or information that is persistent, portable (i.e., is carried *within* the individual), accessible (can be retrieved when needed), and, in the best cases, is usable in a wide array of contexts (what is often called "transfer"). Thus even "simple" skills or concepts we take for granted, such as knowing the answer to 2 + 2= ___, require memories that we continue to carry with us, that we can retrieve immediately, and that we can use to know that adding two cookies to two cookies results in the same number of treats as adding two brussels sprouts to two brussels sprouts.

The portability of memory is a result of the storage of information and skills within our brains. Exactly how the memory is stored will be discussed in depth later, but for now it should be sufficient to note that the process of modifying the brain such that a memory may be accessed for a long period of time is called "consolidation" and the property of the brain and its individual cells that facilitate this process is referred to as "plasticity."

Instruction (i.e., pedagogy) thus leads to changes in the brain (plasticity) that then result in learning that is observable (i.e., performance). Though learning certainly takes place at times when it isn't being assessed, it is only the observable learning that is of use to the educator wanting to know if a student understands or requires further or different instruction. It is performance that is assessed by so-called "high stakes" tests.

It is these three "Ps," pedagogy, plasticity, and performance, that are the focus of this book. Why are all three needed? Certainly, thousands of teachers have been quite successful without *consciously* focusing upon changes in the brain or how psychological phenomena are involved; however, the seeming unconscious ability to apply what turn out to be sound, research-validated strategies and practices without *knowing* that they are in fact supported by evidence represents the artistry that many teachers possess.

This book deals with how to apply the *science* of pedagogy to direct brain plasticity in such a way that student performance is enhanced for as many students as possible. By employing research-validated, general principles of enhanced learning, more time and energy is freed to teach to varying needs of individuals. For our purposes, curriculum and instruction can be reduced to three sets of questions:

> *Pedagogy*: How is learning of the information being facilitated for all students and therefore increasing the likelihood of meeting the individual needs of each student?
> *Plasticity*: What lasting, portable learning has taken place within the student? How can brain science be used to facilitate brain plasticity?
> *Performance*: How is the learning used and can it be measured, seen, applied, and/or transformed?

Together, an understanding of the interconnectedness of pedagogy (the science of teaching), neuroscience (the science of the brain and plasticity), and cognitive science (the science of paying attention, learning, problem solving, and thinking) provide the teacher with an incredible understanding of what is happening within the brain and how the causes and consequences of behavior are linked.

In this book, the studies and research findings that cognitive researchers and neuroscientists use to understand learning will be described, and the ways in which these findings can be translated into usable classroom strategies will be discussed.

Breathing, sleeping, and other behaviors critical for survival all have their origins in neurochemical and electrical signaling taking place within the brain. However, when people think of what the brain does, such as when calling someone a "brainiac" or commenting on a "brain freeze," they are most often referring to what is collectively referred to as *cognition*. Cognition is the sum total of all mental functions and their role in thinking, believing, feeling, and behaving. Cognitive psychology, which studies cognition, is therefore the science of attention, perception, learning, memory, language, problem solving, decision making, and intelligence.

Information from the outside world, which in this context means everything not already within someone's mind, must first be detected by our senses. What we sense, however, does not occur with exact fidelity to the outside world. In fact, the way something *actually* exists—appears, sounds, smells, feels, and tastes—in nature is not necessarily the same as how we perceive it to be. The disparity between actual reality and *our* reality exists because our brains try to make sense of the information that is provided.

If you and a friend have ever both listened to the same song but cannot agree upon what the words being sung were, you can understand this difference between sensation (the lyrics as they were actually sung in the song) and perception (the words you think you heard). Where we direct our senses is in part a result of attention. Attention, which is often thought of as concentration or focus, in turn can result in learning and subsequent storage of the learned information for future use: memory. These four processes, perception, attention, learning, and memory, are the foundation upon which all higher order cognition (e.g., problem solving, language) is built.

Though cognitive processes are often mentioned in isolation (e.g., "pay attention"; "time to learn"), they are actually interdependent and reliant upon one another. For example, optimal learning requires attention; when we focus on something, we are more likely to remember it than when we don't focus upon it. However, knowledge of where, when, and what to focus upon can require memory (we need to know when reading a textbook that there is something special about highlighted text). Thus prior learning influences attention, which then influences future learning. This interdependence of one cognitive process upon another can make it difficult to understand which process is most responsible for an inability to learn or problem solve. For example, if a student is having problems understanding a concept, it may be because she is distracted, perhaps because she doesn't understand the language being used, or because she is making decisions to not pay attention (which is different from being inadvertently distracted).

Careful elimination of possibilities is thus necessary to find the root cause of the problem and implement the correct strategy to ameliorate it. Whenever possible, this text will delineate how cognitive processes relate to one another and how their individual contributions to performance may be disentangled.

Often times, the idea of intelligence is associated with only one or two cognitive process(es), usually learning and/or memory. For example, contestants on Jeopardy would be classified by most viewers as "intelligent" because of their (the contestants') ability to store and retrieve a number of facts. Though learning and memory *are* markers of intelligence in a general sense, they are not the whole story. Because of the interdependence of cognitive processes, intelligence can be seen as product of the interaction of all cognitive processes, including attention, language, and decision making, used toward being successful in a particular setting.

This definition is closer to the viewpoint expressed by Sternberg (2003) than Gardner (1983), as it focuses upon the achievement of a particular goal rather than problem solving or the products of creative thought *per se*. Though widely acknowledged as being incredibly influential to education and differentiated instruction in particular, Gardner's theories of multiple intelligences are seen here as descriptions of the proclivities or leanings that individuals have rather than particular *intelligences* per se.

This does not diminish Gardner's contributions to modern ideas of intelligence, but rather contextualizes how we will treat the phenomenon of intelligence in this particular text, with a research-driven, cognitive basis that allows one to optimize teaching for humans *in general* rather than trying to appeal to the particular strengths of individual learners at all times.

ONE
The Brain and Behavior

THE BASICS OF THE BRAIN

People are probably more intrigued by the brain and its inner workings than any other internal organ. Indeed, even when we commonly refer to the "heart," as used in the sense such as "affairs of the heart" or "heart strings," we are actually referring to a series of molecular and cellular processes that occur within the brain (romantic, huh?). Though thought of as a unified object, *the* brain is actually an incredibly complicated collection of approximately 100 billion neurons, which are the cells responsible for cognition. In addition to the neurons, there are at least ten times that number of brain-specific support cells (glia) that occur in a number of different varieties, each with a particular role. Though neurons, like glia, also come in many "flavors," structurally speaking, the majority of cells have three well-defined regions: the cell body, the axon, and the dendrites.

The cell body is the command center of the cell, housing all of the organelles (i.e., the structures/organs needed for a cell to survive and thrive) necessary for normal functioning as well as the nucleus, where the genetic instructions for each individual reside. Emanating from the cell body are the axon and dendrites, which allow the neuron to communicate with others. Axons and dendrites branch out from a common, singular trunk and allow one neuron to make connections with up to ten thousand other cells. Being from the Northeast, I am able to spend a good portion of the year walking among virtual, though gigantic, facsimiles of neurons once the leaves have fallen from the trees in autumn. On such a walk, if we are to take a standard oak or elm tree as our model neuron, the barren branches are the dendrites (indeed, the word dendrite comes from the Greek *dendros*, which means tree), the main trunk of the tree represents the cell body and the main portion of the axon, and then a stripped-down version of the root system (the dendrites have substantially more branches than the axon) would double as our axonal branches.

The primary role of the axon is to transmit information from neuron to neuron and the role of the dendrite is to receive that information. The *information* that is transmitted between cells is actually chemical in nature. These specialized chemicals are called neurotransmitters, and you probably have heard of some of them such as dopamine, serotonin, and acetylcholine, and others, though equally important, such as substance P and glutamate, you may not have. Neurotransmitters are released from small buds that are found on the ends of axons (sometimes called boutons or, for those less inclined to brevity, presynaptic terminals). When neurotransmitters are released from the boutons, they cross the space between the axon and the dendrites, which is called a synapse, to then bind to specialized receptacles found on the dendritic equivalent of boutons, which are called spines (they are also known as postsynaptic terminals).

On our autumnal tree model, dendritic spines would correspond to the small bumps that occur where the stems of leaves were once attached to our now-barren tree. Once the neurotransmitter is bound to its specific dendritic receptor (neurotransmitters must bind to their own receptors, thus dopamine can only bind to dopamine receptors; it cannot bind to a serotonin receptor), small gates on the surface of the dendrite then open and allow charged molecules (ions) to enter and leave that cell.

It is this flow of ions that creates the electrical current we associate with the brain. This electrical current, if strong enough, then flows within the cell from the dendrite to the cell body, and if the signal is still present, then through the axon (i.e., an *action potential*). The information which started as a chemical signal *outside* the cell is converted to an electrical signal *within* the cell.

Once the electrical signal (action potential) reaches the end of the axon, it then triggers the release of neurotransmitter from its axons, which will then travel across this new synapse. This release of neurotransmitter is sometimes referred to as "firing" (the term is analogous to a gun, where the bouton is the barrel and the firing of the bullet corresponds to the release of neurotransmitter—though the similarities certainly end there).

Information flows from one cell to another, moving from axon to synapse to dendrite to cell body to axon to synapse and so on. This signaling between cells is what facilitates the communication between all of the brain regions that need to "talk" to one another for cognition to take place. Thus to remember something from your childhood, the necessary cells in specific brain regions must fire upon one another to retrieve the stored memory and then to activate the correct recognition of the sounds and letters required to actually say the answer.

A "tip of the tongue" phenomenon that occurs when you absolutely know that you know something but you just can't quite remember what it is is likely the result of the correct cells not being activated when the information is requested. This can result from insufficient activation of a set of cells (thus there is not enough intracellular electrical activation to cause release of neurotransmitter) or activation of the wrong sets of cells within a pathway (i.e., the information was not stored in the cells that were accessed).

The importance of groups of cells from one region firing upon another cannot be understated given the *structure:function* relationship that exists within the brain. Stated simply, the structure:function relationship indicates that specific parts of the brain have well-defined jobs that they perform. For example, the occipital cortex is responsible for different facets of vision; other parts of the brain cannot and do not replicate this function.

If the part of the brain responsible for a given job is injured in some way, the job cannot be performed. This is why stroke victims, who usually have injuries that cut off the oxygen supply, resulting in neurological damage to portions of the language circuit, must often re-learn how to speak; the language regions have been adversely affected by the stroke.

In order to better understand the structure:function relationships of the brain, we will begin our conversation with its external features. The average adult brain weighs between two and three pounds. Initial examination of the exterior reveals a highly convoluted structure that looks somewhat like the shell of a walnut or a mass of spaghetti. The ripples (gyri; singular: gyrus) and folds (sulci; singular: sulcus) of the brain surface, which is called the *cortex*, are believed to be an evolutionary adaptation that allows a greater amount of brain tissue to fit into a space than would happen were it not folded.

Though we take for granted that most human brains are covered in folded and rippled cortical tissue, many animals, including some rather intelligent ones such as rats and mice, have completely ripple-free, smooth brains (*lissencephalic*). Indeed, in some rare cases, lissencephalic humans are born, though the prognosis for the development and longevity of individuals suffering from such abnormalities is usually poor.

The cortical surface is divided from front (rostral; toward the nose) to back (caudal; toward the tail) into two approximate halves or hemispheres, the left and right hemispheres. Some of the folds and ripples are similar between these two hemispheres while others are quite distinct. The sulci and gyri of normally developed humans will have approximately the same location and appearance on both hemispheres, though there is a fair degree of variation among individuals.

The left and right hemispheres are connected to one another by several bundles of axons. These bundles, the largest of which is the corpus callosum, contain thousands of pathways allowing information from the right hemisphere to be communicated to the left and from the left to the right. It should be noted that this connectivity between the hemispheres is critical for normal brain function.

The cortex is roughly divided into four main regions. Moving from the eyes, over the top of the head, and wrapping around from the back to the sides, the four regions are: the frontal lobe, parietal lobe, temporal lobe, and occipital lobe. We will briefly explore examples of the various functions of some major brain regions here, with more details throughout the text.

Looking down at the brain from above, the frontal lobes make up what is approximately the front half of the brain, with a large, deep fold (the central sulcus) separating them from the parietal lobes, which are situated toward the back (away from the eyes). The frontal lobes are responsible for a number of functions. Broca's area, which is responsible for our ability to produce language, is located on the side of the frontal lobe, more often than not on the left. At the very back of the frontal lobe, directly across from the parietal, is the motor cortex, which is responsible for voluntary control of various muscle groups throughout the body. This is where the command to make a fist or to wave goodbye must originate before being transmitted down the spinal column and via peripheral nerves to the actual muscles responsible for the movement.

Given the importance of emotion for cognition, the particulars of which will be discussed throughout this text, many regions of the frontal and its most forward (anterior or rostral) portion, the prefrontal, cortex are of particular importance to educators. For example, through a complex network of feed-forward and feed-backward connections, the medial (toward the middle), dorsolateral (toward the top of the head and to the side), and ventrolateral (toward the face and to the sides) regions of the frontal lobe work with other portions of the brain, such as the anterior cingulate cortex and the amygdala, to recognize emotions in others and regulate our own emotional responses to situations and people.

Directly caudal to (behind) the frontal lobe is the parietal lobe. At the rostral-most (to the front) portion of the parietal lobe, directly across from the frontal lobe's motor cortex, is a strip of tissue referred to as the somatosensory cortex. The somatosensory cortex is responsible for processing signals from touch receptors throughout our body.

When we feel the smooth skin of a baby's arm or the rough stubble of a chin in need of shaving, the cells in which these sensations are actually processed reside within this portion of the brain. Our sensations of hot and cold and pain are also all processed in this part of the brain. In addition, the parietal lobe is also important for what is known as spatial processing, which allows us to navigate through three-dimensional space, both in reality and using our mind's eye. Related to spatial processing and also subserved by the parietal lobe (though not exclusively) is the ability of humans to understand and perform mathematical computations.

Continuing our exploration of the brain, as we continue to move toward the back along the top of the brain, we next encounter the occipital lobe. The occipital lobe is unique in that this portion of the brain is solely devoted to the processing of visual information. The importance of sight to humans as well as the complexities involved with the actual act of seeing are reflected in the size and exclusivity of this particular region.

Along both sides of the brain, almost situated like a thumb alongside a fist, are the temporal lobes. The temporal lobes are particularly important for learning and memory (as are the so-called medial temporal structures, such as the hippocampus, discussed in the following text), and thus are of critical importance to the educator. In addition to mediating the storage of information, the temporal lobes are also critical for the sense of hearing and for our ability to comprehend language (Wernicke's area).

Lying beneath the cortex are subcortical structures that perform a number of important functions. The anterior cingulate cortex, which is found beneath (in anatomical terms, *inferior* to) the frontal lobes and above (*superior* to) the corpus callosum, is an area that may be involved in many higher-order forms of cognition, such as decision making and planning. Deep within the brain are the hypothalamus and thalamus.

The hypothalamus regulates important motives and drives that are critical for survival, such as when and how much to eat and drink, whether to fight or flee, and mating behaviors. The thalamus is important for processing most forms of sensory information before transmitting messages to the cortex and other regions of the brain.

Within the medial temporal lobe are two subcortical structures that are critical to our ability to learn and retain new information. The conversion of passing bits of information into memories that can last a lifetime (i.e., consolidation) is the purview of the hippocampus and its associated structures such as the parahippocampal gyrus, perirhinal cortex, and the entorhinal cortex. The emotional regulation of memory, in particular our ability to remember situations, things, and people that frighten us, is due to the enhancing effect that the amygdala has upon the hippocampus.

Though we have just examined the specific ways that several lobes and subcortical structures regulate thought, it must be remembered that complex mental processes and behaviors, even seemingly simple tasks such as learning that "inferior" is the same as "under" to anatomists, requires a complex coordination of activity within multiple brain regions and of both the right and the left hemispheres. Just as a simple chord on a guitar requires the synchronous plucking of (at least three) individual notes, simple behaviors also require the synchronous activation of multiple brain regions (though many more than just three are needed).

PLASTICITY

Though the gross location of structures in the brain is fixed at birth, a closer look at the wiring of those structures with one another—the incredible, densely packed networks of axons and dendrites forming synapses with one another—is in fact dynamic and, in many parts of the brain, changes continually. As mentioned earlier, the brain's ability to continue to be modified throughout life is referred to as *plasticity*. The plasticity of the brain allows us to continue to grow as people, with new likes, dislikes, skills, facts, and events constantly being added (and deleted).

Though the brains of children are markedly more plastic than that of adults, this capacity to change the brain persists throughout our lives. Thus, contrary to the old adage, one *is* able to "teach an old dog new tricks," provided that the dog's brain remains plastic (which it does). Indeed, my mentor in graduate school didn't learn to play the saxophone until he had achieved tenure as a professor, a feat usually not achieved until individuals are in their fifth decade of life. Now, several decades later, he plays jazz saxophone (and flute) in several bands, performing throughout the Chicago-land area.

The brain's capacity for continued change has some interesting ramifications for the nature of intelligence. For example, an examination of the brain of one of the world's foremost thinkers of the past two hundred years, Albert Einstein, revealed that compared to dozens of brains from individuals who died at approximately the same age, Einstein's brain was unusual in that there was a sizable expansion of a portion of his parietal lobe. The expansion of brain tissue in this region is of more than passing interest because it is believed to underlie the types of advanced thought that would be associated with higher-level, theoretical physics undertaken and revolutionized by Einstein (Witelson, Kigar, & Harvey, 1999).

Though our first assumption is that this region must be responsible for his genius—that it was a differently (rather than abnormally) developed parietal lobe that made Einstein, well, Einstein—this is not necessarily the case. Indeed, because of the plasticity of the brain, it is possible that due to the type of work and thought that Einstein spent the majority of his life performing and contemplating, that he modified his brain to the extent that has been observed. Or, what is probably the case, his parietal lobes conferred an initial level of mathematical prowess that he then further honed through practice and use. Thus his brain may have started out slightly different and then was modified through repeated use.

Though we will likely never know the exact etiology behind this anatomical difference, the fact that it *could* be the result of modifications conferred through merely thinking a particular way—that such possibilities are reality and not mere science fiction—has incredible ramifications for education.

RESEARCHING THE BRAIN AND BEHAVIOR

An advantage of cognitive and brain research is that the ways that experimental and research data are collected lend themselves readily as so-called best practices because they should have broad applicability. Why is this? The bulk of cognitive and brain research utilize research participants (i.e., subjects) who come from what is commonly referred to as "convenience" samples.

The "convenience" for many researchers comes from the fact that most students who take an introductory class in psychology (sometimes called "General Psychology" or "Introduction to Psychology") are required to either participate in real research studies (usually ranging between one to four hours of participation per semester) or fulfill some type of alternative assignment. Because of this research participation requirement, behavioral scientists have a *convenient* sample of individuals for studying various psychological phenomena.

The point of discussing convenience samples here is that these groups of individuals are, in well-designed studies (which will be the ones discussed in this text), randomly assigned to either experimental or control conditions without any regard for learning styles, prior experiences, whether they had breakfast, and so on. Therefore, most individual differences are not considered or accounted for in advance.

By randomly assigning individuals to one group or another, the theory is that individual differences will be sufficiently distributed across groups, such that it is equally likely for individuals with similar styles to end up in all of the groups. Any differences then associated with these differences should equally contribute to what is called statistical noise in all of the groups, thus canceling each other out. Then, once the data have been collected and analyzed, if an experimental or treatment group is found to have learned something significantly better (or worse) than the control (i.e., untreated or modified) condition, it may be argued that whatever treatment was used had an effect, *in general*, upon individuals. This means that findings from cognitive science reflect those practices, stimuli, variables, and so forth that are likely to have an effect upon the *general* population of *humans*.

It is these general findings that are of use here because they are likely to facilitate increased attention, better learning, and greater application of learned concepts/skills in the *majority* of students. Thus the application of concepts in this book is not antithetical to differentiated instruction but is complementary as it frees the instructor to focus on the minority of students for whom these *collectivistic* practices may not work fully. Though differentiated instruction will not be discussed in this book per se, there are many books that deal with the ideas of differentiation, including ways to identify the strengths, comforts, styles, and so forth of individual students (e.g., Connell, 2005).

What *will* be discussed is what is known about the cognitive phenomena of direct relevance to education, what is known to take place in the brain as a result, and how instruction and curricula can be tailored using this information to meet the needs of the majority of students.

Not surprisingly, most of the ways that cognition is studied are similar to the ways that achievement is assessed in schools. Reaction time, meaning how quickly someone can finish a task, is used as a marker of mastery, where individuals with faster reaction times are seen as having greater mastery or understanding than those with slower reaction times. With cognitive phenomena, differences in reaction time can be measured on the order of minutes, seconds, or even milliseconds (thousandths of a second).

Accuracy is another tried and true measure of cognition. Just as the percentage of responses answered correctly (i.e., *performance*) on an exam is used as a marker of understanding, percent correctly remembered is used as a marker of memory and learning. Similarly, the ability to transfer information learned in one context to another can be measured and assessed using various means.

It is presumed that all behavioral changes are the result of brain modifications (plasticity), be they molecular, synaptic, structural, or collectivistic. How do we know that such changes actually take place? Anatomical changes, such as those that accompany learning, are examined in a number of ways. The most direct way to examine brain changes is by studying the actual brain tissue itself. By carefully sectioning the post-mortem brain tissue of humans and animals into incredibly thin slices (usually on the order of 1–40 micrometers[1]), different dyes and markers can be used to examine changes in the physical structure of brain cells, modifications to how they connect to one another, and increases or decreases in the different molecules that mediate those changes.

For example, when Aryeh Routtenberg, Marcel Mesulam, Brian Quinn, and I were interested in how the brains of patients who suffered from Alzheimer's disease differed from those who didn't, we examined 40-micrometer sections of brain tissue from the hippocampus using special markers that would bind to the molecule we were interested in examining (Rekart et al., 2004).

Using this method, we found an increased quantity of the marker in the hippocampus of patients who suffered from Alzheimer's disease, therefore suggesting the presence of greater quantities of the molecule we were interested in, which in this case was a protein responsible for the growth of axons, GAP-43. Based on the amount of the marker for GAP-43 and the location of the increases, we were able to hypothesize that though much of the memory loss associated with Alzheimer's disease is due to cell death, there may also be a memory consequence, possibly confusion, from compensatory growth processes that we observed from a redirection of connections among surviving cells (i.e., reactive synaptogenesis).

Large-scale structural changes can be observed using imaging techniques such as magnetic resonance imaging, or MRI, which allows researchers to examine the brains of humans without having to remove them first. Furthermore, actual brain activity can be studied using a modification of this technique, *functional* MRI, or fMRI. When an individual is examined using fMRI, changes in the quantity of different markers of activity, such as blood oxygen levels (BOLD), provide clues regarding the parts of the brain that are involved in the performance of a task.

For example, while being scanned in an fMRI instrument, an individual could be asked to read three different words (e.g., FACE, TABLE, and GAME) and determine what one word could create three new items when added to each of the existing words. If the person came up with "CARD," which would result in "FACE CARD," "CARD TABLE," and "CARD GAME," then there would be a spike in the level of blood oxygen in the right superior temporal gyrus, indicating that this region is somehow involved in such "Aha" moments of insight (Jung-Beeman et al., 2004). But how is this one region detected on the scan when in fact an incredibly large number of regions distributed across the entire brain are also active, regardless if the word "CARD" pops into one's mind or not?

In order to "see" the regions that are *differentially* active when someone comes up with a correct answer, multiple trials in the fMRI scanner are run, with the hope that on some of the trials (i.e., background) the participant will fail to come up with the correct word. Put differently, the activation in the brain for the words FACE, TABLE, and GAME when "CARD" was successfully identified would be subtracted from the activation for the trio of HOT, CODE, and WINE when the word "RED" was not.

Whenever results from brain imaging are discussed, it must be remembered that regions identified as being "activated" are only those that differ from all of the other regions that are *normally* active and that help us to carry out all the myriad and sundry tasks required of the brain on a continuous basis. Though fMRI is a powerful technique, what it doesn't answer is whether a particular region is critical for the successful completion of the task (e.g., coming up with the word "CARD") or not. This means that we don't know if the right superior temporal gyrus is actually involved in finding the correct answer, recognizing that the answer is correct, or processing a feeling of success (or relief) at coming up with an answer.

In addition to monitoring where blood oxygen levels are changing within the brain, neuroscientists can also examine communication within the brain as it is happening. Remember that the brain relies on both electrical (inside individual neurons) and chemical (between neurons; neurotransmitters) signaling to facilitate cognition. Electrical signaling from the cortical surfaces of the brain, sometimes called "brain waves," can be monitored using a series of surface electrodes used in electroencephalography, or EEG.

Though an entire neuron is electrically polarized, EEGs only detect what happens at the dendritic terminal when neurotransmitters cause ions to enter the cell (evoked potentials) and do not pick up the action potentials associated with the release of neurotransmitter at the very end of the axons. The measurement of surface brain waves can be quite robust and in fact is commonly used in many newborn hearing screens.

One of two main tests for hearing function in newborn babies, the auditory brainstem response (ABR), allows doctors to know months before a child ever says a word whether s/he has hearing problems. To detect the ABR, small speakers are placed near the ears of the infant. When sounds are projected from the speakers, the corresponding brain waves from the auditory system will be detected by small electrodes (they look somewhat like modified Band-Aids) and displayed on a computer screen if the child has normal hearing.

The detection of chemical signaling between neurons is slightly more difficult than measuring communication within individual groups of cells as is done with EEG. Positron emission tomography, or PET, is a technique that lets neuroscientists (academic brain researchers, usually holding a PhD) and neurologists (medical doctors specializing in the brain and its disorders) determine where and when specific neurotransmitters are binding. This is accomplished through the use of short-lived, radioactive molecules (radiotracers) that are ingested by the research subject or patient.

The radiotracer is transported into the brain and then binds to specific receptors where they can then be detected by the PET imager, allowing an approximate picture of the location of some neurotransmitter receptor sites as well as how "full" the sites are at a given point in time. Neurotransmitter sites that are less "full" with the individual's own neurotransmitters (i.e., those that aren't radioactive) will be able to bind more of the radiotracer. In contrast, when something has caused a large increase in the release of neurotransmitter, the receptor sites are too full with non-radioactive neurotransmitter to allow much of the radiotracer to be bound, and, thus, there is little to no radioactive signal to detect.

Though, classically, many of these techniques were used separately, modern neuroscientists have developed methods for using many of the techniques concurrently, thus providing a fuller picture (literally) of the brain and how it works when we are engaged in various types of cognition.

FINAL THOUGHTS: LIMITATIONS OF RESEARCH

The scope of what researchers can accomplish is limited in many ways. Remember the convenience sampling discussed earlier? Though ideally researchers would assess the learning and cognition of a representative sample of people, meaning one that best captures the breadth and diversity of humanity, in practice this is hardly ever the case.[2] Furthermore, most if not all brain and cognitive researchers conduct their analyses in laboratory settings, where as many variables are identified and controlled as possible. Compared to the control of a laboratory, a classroom is filthy with variables of many types.

Why should the distinction between the control of variables and other factors in laboratories and classrooms matter? Put simply, it matters because "evidence-based" is often mistakenly interpreted as meaning the same thing as "field-tested." To say that a particular teaching strategy or curricular initiative is "evidence-based" can indicate many things. It certainly may mean, *as most assume*, that the phenomenon has been studied in classroom settings by educational researchers and teachers and has been found to work. And if this latter situation is the case, great! However, more often than not this label means that a particular educational strategy or initiative is based on evidence that has emerged from research studies conducted in *laboratories, or it is based in evidence*.

There is certainly nothing wrong with this other definition and I also do not believe that it is *intentionally* used to deceive. Indeed, many of the strategies proposed in this text represent exactly this *type* of research-based practice, namely those that have yet to be tested in classroom settings. However, any time you come across something that is research-based rather than research-*validated* (or field-tested), remember that the minimum threshold for this label is that the strategy is based on a review of the existing literature. Thus it is "field-tested" or "research-validated" and not "evidence-based" that should be seen as the educational equivalent of the "Good Housekeeping" stamp of approval.

Finally, even stating that something is research-based suggests that there is something about the particular standards that research is held to that should confer confidence. Indeed, there is a procedure in place to ensure that research that will be published meets a rigorous standard, namely the peer-review process. For a journal to be peer-reviewed means that the articles that are published have been reviewed and accepted by a group of outside experts (usually three to four).

The experts are individuals who have themselves published on the subject of the article, and these individuals may come from anywhere in the world. The act of peer review involves agreeing to review the article (nowadays most reviewers are contacted electronically by an editor via email), reading the article, and writing a detailed critique, which includes the pros, cons, and overall recommendation (usually "accept," "accept with revisions," "revise and resubmit," or "reject") with an explanation for the recommendation.

All in all, the entire process takes anywhere from four to twelve hours and is done entirely for free. Yes, that's correct; peer reviewers donate their time for the good of science. There are several reasons why this practice is conducted pro bono publico; however, one of the most important is so that there is no financial incentive for reviewers to accept or reject a particular article.

Now, though on the surface this may seem like a fantastic system—and indeed, it is the best one that currently exists—it does not always work as planned. One issue is the fact that there are, at least in education, over one hundred different journals. These journals cover a wide array of topics from administration to special education. Within a particular subarea of education, such as administration, there is a hierarchy of journals based on the quality of the research published within those volumes (this same class system exists throughout the social and natural sciences, with some journals seen as being better than others).

There can be, though not always, an association between the quality of the research and the quality of the journal. Unfortunately, though there is some agreement about the best journals, there is little consensus regarding which metrics to use (e.g., the average number of times that a paper published in a particular journal is cited by other authors) to determine the quality of what are seen as second- and third-tier journals. Furthermore, even in the best journals there are occasions when research with flawed methodologies is published despite the peer-review process. How does this occur? In part, it may be due to reviewers pushing personal agendas vis-à-vis a particular set of findings. That is to say, if a submitted manuscript has findings that reinforce or support the reviewer's own work, s/he is probably more likely to accept the manuscript than if the findings are a contradiction.

In addition, as already indicated, the peer-review process is conducted by academics for free. It stands to reason that for academics whose schedules are filled with papers to grade, grants to write, results to interpret, classes to teach, and so forth that reviewing an article falls fairly low on the priority list. I know from personal experience that items moved to the proverbial back burner are completed whenever a small chunk of time presents itself, which admittedly may result in a rushed or less-than-fantastic job. Sometimes methodological flaws or other issues that can confound research may be overlooked during the review process. Though the reliance on multiple reviewers should prevent this from happening, it is not always the case.

Finally, even when an article appears in a "good" journal and the research methods are sound, one should examine the actual study itself before passing any judgment about the applicability of the results. For example, when I was in graduate school I became aware of a well-publicized study suggesting that people who drank coffee had a lower likelihood of developing Parkinson's disease (PD) than non-coffee drinkers (Ross et al., 2000).

Like many graduate students, I was particularly fond of my morning, afternoon, evening, and nightly cups of coffee; indeed, coffee was by far my favorite vehicle for feeding my addiction to caffeine. After finding out that the research was published in the prestigious *Journal of the American Medical Association*, or "JAMA," I decided to see what the researchers actually found.

Unfortunately after reading the article, which was conducted on Japanese Americans (which I am not) in Hawaii (where I do not nor have ever lived), I realized that there were too many dissimilarities between myself and the sample (which was not randomly selected) for me to start touting my coffee habit as a healthy lifestyle. Though subsequent studies with other populations of individuals have produced similar results (Costa et al., 2010), much to my delight, at the time there wasn't sufficient evidence to make the connection between the behavior (coffee drinking) and the result (prevention of Parkinson's disease).

This discussion of the limitations of research should not leave us with nihilistic feelings about research. On the contrary, it should confirm that research is a living, evolving, *human* enterprise. What fails to be supported today may be found to be the next best thing tomorrow—such is the nature of scientific inquiry. Rather, this discussion is meant to instill a healthy sense of skepticism about claims, which abound, regarding "strategy X" being "evidence" or "research-based."

In the context of the chapters and pages that follow, I will indicate and provide the sources for all research findings that are used. The studies that are described within have been examined with a critical eye not just by the peer reviewers and editors but by me. Furthermore, the phenomena that will have the greatest credibility as being viable, usable strategies for general education will be those that have been replicated by multiple laboratories in different settings and/or those that have actually been field-tested and research-validated in classroom or other educational settings. Such findings will be used as a springboard for launching best practices that use sound pedagogy to facilitate brain plasticity and create real, observable performance increases in today's students.

POINTS TO REMEMBER

- Educators are *applied* cognitive scientists.
- Pedagogy leads to lasting changes in the structure of the brain (plasticity), which is measured using some indicator of performance.

- The brain consists of billions of cells called neurons that are responsible for cognition.
- Neurons have three distinct parts. The axon is what sends information to other cells, the dendrite is what receives information, and the cell body, or soma, is where the determination is, where incoming information is processed and a choice is made to either pass it along to other cells or not.
- Information passes between neurons in the form of chemical messengers called neurotransmitters. Information that travels within a cell from dendrite to axon is electrical.
- There is a structure:function relationship in the brain. Specific areas of the brain are responsible for particular behaviors and cognitive processes.
- The brain maintains the ability to be modified and enhanced throughout one's life. This process, called plasticity, is responsible for the lasting changes that accompany education.
- Cognition is the sum total of all mental functions and their role in thinking, believing, feeling, and behaving. Attention, perception, learning, memory, language, decision making, and problem solving are all cognitive processes.
- There are many ways in which cognition can be examined. These range from simple learning tasks to the imaging of the brain as it works using sophisticated methods, such as fMRI, PET, and electroencephalography (EEGs).
- The word "research" is used in this text to refer to the process of systematically examining a phenomenon using the scientific method. Research-based practices are desirable because of the peer-review process.
- Research-based and research-validated practices are not identical. Any practice that is based on findings from studies conducted in controlled, laboratory settings is research-based. Though these findings may lead to effective classroom strategies, it is not assured. Research-validated practices, on the other hand, have been shown to work in real classrooms.

NOTES

1. One micrometer is equivalent to approximately four hundred-thousandths of an inch.

2. Though political scientists do a better job than most at obtaining representative samples for opinion polls.

REFERENCES

Connell, J. D. (2005). *Brain-based strategies to reach every learner: Surveys, questionnaires, and checklists that help you identify students' strengths-plus engaging brain-based lessons and activities.* Danbury, CT: Scholastic.

Costa, J., Lunet, N., Santos, C., Santos, J., & Vaz-Carneiro, A. (2010). Caffeine exposure and the risk of Parkinson's Disease: A systematic review and meta-analysis of observational studies. *Journal of Alzheimer's Disease, 20,* 221–238.

Friedman, T. L. (2005). *The world is flat: A brief history of the twenty-first century.* New York: Farrar, Straus, & Giroux.

Gardner, H. (1983/2003). *Frames of mind: The theory of multiple intelligences.* New York: Basic Books.

Jung-Beeman, M., Bowden, E. M., Haberman, J., Frymiare, J. L., Arambel-Liu, S., Greenblatt, R., Reber, P. J., & Kounios, J. (2004). Neural activity observed in people solving verbal problems with insight. *Public Library of Science—Biology, 2,* 500–510.

Ravitch, D. (2010). *The death and life of the great American school system: How testing and choice are undermining education.* New York: Basic Books.

Rekart, J. L., Quinn, B., Mesulam, M., & Routtenberg, A. (2004). Subfield-specific increase in brain growth protein in postmortem hippocampus of Alzheimer's patients. *Neuroscience, 126*(3), 579–584.

Rosen, H. J., & Levenson, R. W. (2009). The emotional brain: Combining insights from patients and basic science. *Neurocase, 15*(3), 173–181.

Ross, G. W., Abbott, R. D., Petrovitch, H., Morens, D. M., Grandinetti, A., Tung, K-H., Tanner, C. M., Masaki, K. H., Blanchette, P. L., Curb, J. D., Popper, J. S., & White, L. R. (2000). Association of coffee and caffeine intake with the risk of Parkinson's disease. *Journal of the American Medical Association, 283,* 2674–2679.

Sternberg, R. J. (2003). A broad view of intelligence: A theory of successful intelligence. *Consulting Psychology Journal: Practice and Research, 55,* 139–154.

Witelson, S. F., Kigar, D. L., & Harvey, T. (1999). The exceptional brain of Albert Einstein. *The Lancet, 353,* 2149–2153.

TWO
Perception

There is an entire world of experiences that we, as humans, will never know. Unfortunately, there is no solution for this ignorance as it is deeply rooted in our biology. I know this may seem an odd way to begin a chapter in a book about education, but it accurately captures the tone of this chapter. Namely, that there is the world that exists as it actually *is* and then there is the world as we *experience it*. Put differently, if we look to other animals, we know that some have better sight (though not many), others better hearing, and most mammals, better senses of smell.

Snakes experience a world of heat, with infrared detection, that goes unnoticed by us. Similarly, the world to a dog is a complex tapestry of various odors and scents. These differences between the collective "them" and "us" are rooted in our ability to decipher clues from the environment.

BASICS OF PERCEPTION

The process of understanding what is happening around us begins with our senses, such as vision and audition (hearing), which psychologists place under the umbrella term of "sensation." Sensation refers to how different forms of energy, such as light or sound, are translated into neural signals (i.e., electrical signals and neurotransmitter release) that can be understood by the brain (i.e., transduction). As any third grader can tell you, we have more than just two senses, but for the purposes of this text, we will largely ignore touch, smell, and taste.

Though these latter three senses are each fascinating in their own right, we will focus upon the perception of visual and auditory stimuli because these are the two senses that are primarily used in standard academic settings. Furthermore, we will expand the standard definition of perception so that it encompasses more than just the brain's interpretation of sensory information, to include our perceptions of emotion and time.

We will largely ignore our sense of touch as well as the way we detect where our body is in three-dimensional space (i.e., even if I close my eyes, I am aware of my fingers being outstretched on the keyboard of my laptop; proprioception). This is important because this also means that we will not be paying any mind to what is often called "kinesthetic" learning. Though some learning style theorists posit that there are "kinesthetic" learners, as we will see in our discussions of encoding and retrieval, the "visual," "auditory," and "kinesthetic" (VAK) labels do not have any actual basis in brain or cognitive research (e.g., Goswami, 2006).

Though neither "auditory" nor "visual" learning styles are actually valid labels or descriptors of true differences, these at least tap directly into actual sensory modalities. A kinesthetic learning style, were it to exist, would not be very effective as the types of direct connectivity that are observed between visual and auditory centers are not found in the tactile modality. Neither the somatosensory cortices, the brain regions responsible for processing touch information, nor the cerebellum, the brain region that facilitates some forms of motor learning, would produce the type of long-term, transferable learning that is desirable in academic settings.

So, let's get back to what we *will* be discussing. Vision is the sense that detects light. The light that we can observe is actually a very narrow stretch of about 400–700 nanometers of the much larger electromagnetic spectrum. Outside this narrow band exist frequencies that are detected by other animals, such as infrared (snakes) and ultraviolet (honeybees) light. Furthermore, at the extreme ends of the spectrum are relatively useful and harmless energies like radio waves and those that should be avoided (particularly by physicists named "Bruce"), gamma waves.

Vision begins when light enters the eye through its aperture (i.e., the pupil). Light then travels through the aqueous humor located in the front portion of the eye, through the lens, which focuses and projects light energy through the vitreous humor and onto the posterior surface where it is absorbed by special cells at the back of the retina called rods and cones. The absorption of light by rods and cones causes a chemical reaction to occur within these cells that causes a change in their release of neurotransmitters onto other cells in the retina called bipolar cells.

Once activated, bipolar cells then release neurotransmitters onto retinal ganglion cells, whose axons, which make up the optic nerve, leave the eye and interface with the brain. Visual information is transmitted from the eye through the axons of the retinal ganglion cells. With the exit of information from the eye, the act of sensation is complete and the brain now engages in perceiving what the signal is.

Perception

Perception is an interpretive process, which involves reconstructing a signal and interpreting what it is. Light signals that higher-order centers of the brain receive are different from the signals that were detected by the eye. Differences arise because the brain uses existing information from experience to influence how we interpret what we are seeing.

When I was in graduate school, I had a large, tabby-colored Maine Coon named "Yukon Cornelius" who would sit up with me at night while I worked on articles or analyzed data (an exciting life, to be sure). Yukon was quite considerate and wouldn't try to sit in my lap while I was working (which would have been difficult given his considerable girth at 24 pounds) but preferred instead to straddle the arm of a couch that was near where I was working.

It was quite a sight to see this incredibly large feline dangling two legs from either side of the arm of a couch. Our routine, me working late into the night and him keeping me company from his perch, went on for over a decade. The point of this story is that although he had to be euthanized due to kidney failure (he was 19) in 2008, there are times at night when it seems as though he is visiting me.

Yes, you read that last line correctly. OK, so he doesn't *really* visit me, but on occasion I still *see* him, though only for a moment. I still work late at night and every so often a couch cushion or one of my children's toys will be propped up against or resting on the arm of the couch. When it is late and the light is dim, there are times when I look quickly in the direction of the couch and it seems as though I see, for just a moment, my deceased cat sitting on the arm.

Lasting no more than a second, the image of Yukon is a prime example of what happens when our eyes take in information (sensation) and our brain, not knowing how to interpret it, uses the best "fit" that it can (perception). In this example, my eyes detect a large, dark lump on the corner of the couch. My brain, trying to make sense of what the dark lump could be, searches through past experiences/memories to find a match. And, based on the years we spent together, my brain for a moment interprets the shady lump as a cat before it realizes that the possibility is impossible and it moves on to other options.

This example illustrates how visual perception is influenced by the brain's use of old information (i.e., experience) to try and find a match for new information (i.e., what is being sensed). The same situation holds for our sense of hearing as well. Unlike vision, which occurs due to the chemical transduction of light energy into release of neurotransmitter, hearing is caused by changes in pressure that result in the microscopic bending of hair-like appendages of specialized cells.

Beginning at the outer ear, sounds waves, which are really nothing more than pressure fluctuations in the air that surrounds us, cause vibrations in the eardrum (i.e., tympanic membrane). The eardrum then, in a fashion that Rube Goldberg would appreciate, vibrates three small bones (i.e., ossicles): the hammer, the anvil, and the stirrup. The hammer, which is connected to the interior of the ear drum, then moves back and forth, in turn causing the anvil to move, which in turn, moves the stirrup. The stirrup then vibrates yet another membrane, similar to the eardrum (i.e., the oval window), that causes the fluid in our inner ear, which is a structure called the cochlea, to move.

Embedded within the cochlea are thousands of small hair cells that sit just under a membrane. When the fluid in our inner ears is in motion, this causes the membrane to brush lightly against the hair cells, which, in turn, bends them. The microscopic bends in these tiny hairs cause the release of neurotransmitter (sensation), which is transmitted via the auditory nerve to the brain (perception). Just as with vision, auditory perception also relies on memory to make judgments about what we are hearing at any given moment.

These brief descriptions of how information from the outside world is processed show how sensory information is broken down in our ears and eyes before it is reassembled by the brain. Thus though we see with our eyes and hear with our ears, the sights and sounds that we *actually* experience are not identical to what was originally heard or seen. Rather, our perceptual experiences are the byproduct of complex reassembly processes that take place in a number of brain structures, including the visual and auditory cortices, which are heavily influenced by interpretation and past experiences.

VISUAL IMAGERY

Did you ever wonder why you have to close your eyes to imagine something? This is because many of the same structures used to see the world are also recruited when we imagine something (Ganis, Thompson, & Kosslyn, 2004). Because the same circuitry is involved in both seeing and imagining, it is only when we remove interference from actual visual input from the eyes that we can focus on the images from our mind's "eyes." Indeed, this overlap of circuitry means that when we imagine something our brain even treats the image as though it had the same properties that a real object that exists somewhere in the world would have.

Shepard and Metzler (1971) demonstrated this phenomenon by having participants view three-dimensional block-like objects (think of the game Tetris). Participants were presented with two of these objects simultaneously and were asked if they were the same. Some of the objects were the same; however, because the two objects were presented at different angles, to determine if they were the same or different, one would have to mentally rotate one or both of the objects.

What the researchers found was that there was a linear relationship between the amount of rotation necessary to determine if the two objects were the same and the amount of time it took for participants to identify the two objects as the same. So if one object required 45 degrees of rotation to resemble the other, it took significantly less time for participants to recognize that the two were the same than if the same object had to be rotated 135 degrees to make that determination.

These findings and others like them are important as they show us how the brain treats imagined objects. Just as it takes longer to align two objects that are 135 degrees different than 45, so does it take longer for our brain to rotate the *virtual* objects. Though this finding may seem like common sense, it was a critical demonstration that showed that it doesn't just seem as though we are rotating the objects in our mind as though they are real, we really are.

How does the brain facilitate our ability to *act* on virtual objects as though they are real? Though there are many regions involved in this process, including an area called the parietal operculum, our concern here is on the recruitment of the visual cortex. As indicated earlier, just as the visual cortex is used to actually see what exists outside of us, it is also used to *see* what our minds create. This dual role has some interesting ramifications.

For one, it confers upon us the ability to visualize objects that aren't actually present with a fair amount of detail. This benefit comes at a cost, however. Because the system we use to imagine objects relies on the same neural machinery needed to actually view objects, there is a limit to what and how much information can be processed simultaneously.

Regardless of whether the image begins within us or from outside, there are only so many neurons and synapses that can be activated at one point in time. Furthermore, there is only one *mind's eye*, our virtual projection screen upon which we perceive stimuli. This is why if you've ever been driving while deeply engrossed in your thoughts, which probably involved some mental images, you may have felt as though your car "drove itself" to your destination. This dissociation from the conscious processing of stimuli (they are still processed, though at a lower, less detail-oriented level, otherwise how did you get to work or wherever else you were going) is the result of your choice to focus your attention (more on this in the next chapter) on your thoughts rather than the road.

In the classroom, we must be conscious of the competition between a student's internal thoughts and whatever we are presenting. Daydreaming has a much more insidious learning cost for visual information than auditory if it involves images (we can have interference that also uses our *mind's voice and ear* in a similar fashion; see chapter 4). Similarly, if we are asking students to "picture something" or perform some other feat of imagination, we must be cognizant of the fact that we should not be simultaneously presenting slide shows or images related to concepts that we want our students to retain.

MIRRORING OF BEHAVIOR

As a new parent, there is no greater feeling than when your infant looks back at you with what seems to be recognition and matches the smile on your face with one of her own. This "mirroring" back of our own joy and emotion is interpreted by us in many different ways. "She knows who I am," "she loves me," and "she is so happy" are all interpretations that we may make based on the child's outward behavior.

These little moments in which a parent and child acknowledge each other and share a positive emotional experience will then set the stage for later social communication that the child will have. The parent's joy at the child's behavior only seeks to increase the likelihood of the little one behaving the same way again. Just as a pigeon who is rewarded with a morsel of food for pushing a lever will continue to do so, so too will the child who is rewarded with affection and positive regard continue with the antecedent behaviors.

Many animals, in addition to humans, have an innate need to *mirror* the behaviors of others. For humans, this has enormous repercussions for parents and teachers alike. It turns out that there are specialized neurons within our brains, called *mirror neurons*, that become active when others perform activities (Rizzolatti & Sinigaglia, 2010). These neurons are responsible for our sensory processes as well as those responsible for our movements. This is why if you've ever seen somebody stub his toe, you wince in pain. The uncontrollable urge you have to wince is the result of neural activity in pain neurons from your toe that become activated when you view someone else harm his. Similarly, when you see somebody pick up a cup, the neurons in your brain responsible for sending messages to the muscles in your fingers and thumbs to grasp will become activated as well (only a subset, otherwise whenever we observe people doing things we would involuntarily mime the same actions).

The existence of the mirror neuron system supports the importance of modeling as an instructional tool. Indeed, it suggests that by demonstrating particular actions or behaviors, we may be priming the brains of those who are observing us to perform the same behaviors on their own. The mirror neuron system also suggests, and indeed this is the case as we will soon see, that there must be a mechanism that allows us to know when we are being instructed and by whom.

THE SPECIAL ROLE OF FACES

A few years ago, American Express put out a commercial (searchable on YouTube as "Don't Take Chances: Take Charge") that didn't contain a single living creature. Despite the fact that no animate objects, drawings, or paintings were displayed, the one-minute advertisement nonetheless contained twenty-four distinct faces. The early faces that are shown are quite sad, but as the commercial progresses (and the benefits of the product being advertised are extolled) the faces become much happier. Some of the faces are cuter than others and each has its own personality. So how does a commercial that doesn't actually have faces do all of this?

The makers of the commercial sagely used images of everyday objects that they knew would be interpreted as faces. Each picture that was presented thus had two objects in the place where we would expect there to be eyes and then some kind of a shape to represent the mouth. For example, one of the images was the top of a frothy mug of cocoa. The circle formed by the top of the mug provided the outline of the face, and within the mug there was froth missing in three areas: two small circles, which gave the impression of eyes, and a line under those circles that suggested a thinly drawn mouth in the form of a frown. The beauty of the commercial is that though we *know* that there aren't any actual faces being presented, the emotional content conveyed by each is unmistakable. Indeed, the viewer has no choice but to *see* the face.

Within the brain, a specialized area of the temporal cortex facilitates our perception of faces. The fusiform face area, or FFA, recognizes various shapes and objects and binds them together so that faces emerge, even where they don't actually exist (Kanwisher, McDermott, & Chun, 1997). Given the incredible number of tasks for which the brain is responsible, everything from breathing to the release of hormones to falling in love, it is striking that an entire region of the brain would have evolved specifically and arguably, solely, to recognize faces. Indeed, the existence of specialized brain areas, such as the FFA, speak to how evolutionarily important face recognition must be for human beings as social animals (Kanwisher, 2010).

Working with the FFA is the superior temporal sulcus (STS), which is responsible for directing our gaze toward others and following where others are looking (Frischen, Bayliss, & Tipper, 2007). Together, the STS and FFA are responsible for our recognition of when people are looking at us—an ability that develops in infancy and helps to engage our attention throughout life. Eye contact is important for other cognitive processes, like learning, because our attention is captured when someone makes eye contact with us (Frischen, Bayliss, & Tipper, 2007).

The importance of eye contact cannot be overstated. As a nonverbal social cue, eye contact contributes a great deal of information. Though making eye contact and holding one's gaze is seen as an aggressive behavior by many species, it often has quite the opposite effect in humans. Humans actually have a larger degree of white tissue (the sclera) surrounding the colored iris and darkened pupil than is found in other primates, which may facilitate our ability to follow one's gaze and know where exactly s/he is looking (Frischen, Bayliss, & Tipper, 2007).

Eye contact and gaze perception, which are impaired in children with autism spectrum disorders, are important, hard-wired behaviors that are typically found in developing children and adults (Senju & Johnson, 2009). Since these behaviors provide important social and affective cues, they are likely to be important components of the nonverbal dynamic that is established between a teacher and students.

The cohort of such behaviors, which communicate caring and stability to students, have been placed under the umbrella term of teacher *immediacy* (Mehrabian, 1968). The frequency and distribution of eye contact (i.e., with one student or the entire class), is used as a marker of effective teaching in at least one modern teacher evaluation system (e.g., Marzano, Frontier, & Livingstone, 2011). So, is there evidence that eye contact actually impacts learning?

Interestingly, despite its anecdotal reputation for being a critical mediator of a successful teacher:student relationship, there is a relative dearth of experimental examinations (i.e., the kind that can actually show a causal relationship between teacher eye contact and student learning) of the actual contribution that eye contact makes to academic success. One study that directly examined the manipulation of eye contact upon student learning (as well as what was called "physical immediacy," which refers to the placement of a desk or other object between the teacher and students, teacher posture, etc.) did find that students had better short-term learning (long-term learning wasn't examined) when the instructor maintained good eye contact throughout the lecture (Kelley & Gorham, 1988).

Certainly, the aforementioned finding is encouraging; however, there are several methodological issues that bear mention. First, students were "taught" on a one-to-one basis during the study. Second, the learning task involved the memorization of strings of six (total) words and numbers, such as "house, 20, bat, 31, stick, 92" (Kelley & Gorham, 1988, p. 202). Thus neither the "classroom" environment in the study nor the information to be learned adequately mimics the complex environment of the average K–12 classroom. However, with these caveats in mind, it *was* found that participants in the low eye contact condition made significantly greater errors related to the order of words and numbers, which suggests that a lack of eye contact may divide attention between the incoming stimuli (i.e., what is to be learned) and the unconscious desire to know where the speaker is looking (see chapter 3 for more on divided attention).

Most of the studies that have examined eye contact have examined students' perceptions of how well they would learn (i.e., answering questions like how well one agrees or disagrees with the statement "I could learn a great deal from this teacher" after the nonverbal and verbal tendencies of the teacher have been described) with a particular teacher rather than actual learning outcomes. Students across cultures (i.e., Finland, Puerto Rico, Australia, and the United States) reliably indicate that they feel as though they would learn more from teachers who use effective immediacy behaviors. And the nonverbal behavior routinely rated as one of the most important is eye contact (McCroskey et al., 1996).

Although most studies do indicate that nonverbal behaviors such as eye contact do influence student learning, there is no consensus as to how much of a difference these behaviors actually make (Witt, Wheeless, & Allen, 2006). Regardless of the actual direct relationship to student learning, the fact that students' perceptions about teachers and their own prospects for learning are enhanced by nonverbal behaviors, such as making and maintaining good eye contact, should be cause enough to make sure that such good pedagogical techniques are utilized frequently.

EMOTIONS AND PERCEPTION

Emotions are the complex representations of how we feel, how our bodies respond, and how we behave throughout life. Relatively short-lived, emotions are high in intensity (*moods* are the longer-lived, less intense cousin of emotions). Psychologically, emotions consist of two components: *valence* and *arousal*. Valence has to do with our subjective assessment or what we commonly refer to as feelings. It is a continuum from positive (those feelings that are pleasurable and that we choose to experience) to negative (those that are aversive and that we seek to avoid). Most of us have an intuitive sense of what it means for an emotion to be positive or negative, with happy falling on the positive side and sad being negative.

Arousal is a measure of the degree of the excitability that the emotion evokes. Arousal can be seen as a continuum from high arousal, with a great deal of excitability and physiological activation, to low arousal, whereby the individual is conscious, but barely so. Emotions that are opposite in arousal would be *excited* and *calm*. Though there is broad agreement that emotion consists of *at least* these two dimensions, some psychological researchers maintain that arousal may be further divided into separate dimensions (Rafaeli & Revelle, 2006).

These researchers maintain that the two types of arousal are *energetic arousal* and *tense arousal*. Energetic arousal is consistent with the definition given previously and is a reflection of physiological activation. Tense arousal, on the other hand, refers more to what may be thought of as "nervous energy" and is related to anxiety. Though there is some evidence that in fact two independent arousal dimensions do exist (Rekart, Rekart, & Bizeur, 2008), we will lump both together for our purposes using the umbrella term of *arousal*.

The two dimensions of emotion can be demonstrated graphically by placing valence on a hypothetical x-axis and arousal on a hypothetical y-axis (Russell, 1980; see Figure 2.1. All emotions that we experience, then, are varying combinations of arousal and valence. We can think of "sad" as being negatively valenced, with moderate to low levels of arousal and "distraught" as being even more negatively valenced and higher in arousal.

Some emotions are experienced and expressed similarly across cultures. These emotions, referred to as "basic," are found across the planet and have stereotyped facial expressions and behaviors associated with them. For example, if you were to encounter someone you didn't know and she had raised eyebrows, wide-open eyes, and her mouth were agape, you would likely infer that she was frightened. It doesn't matter if you and she speak the same language, have the same cultural norms, and so forth, you would still know what she was feeling.

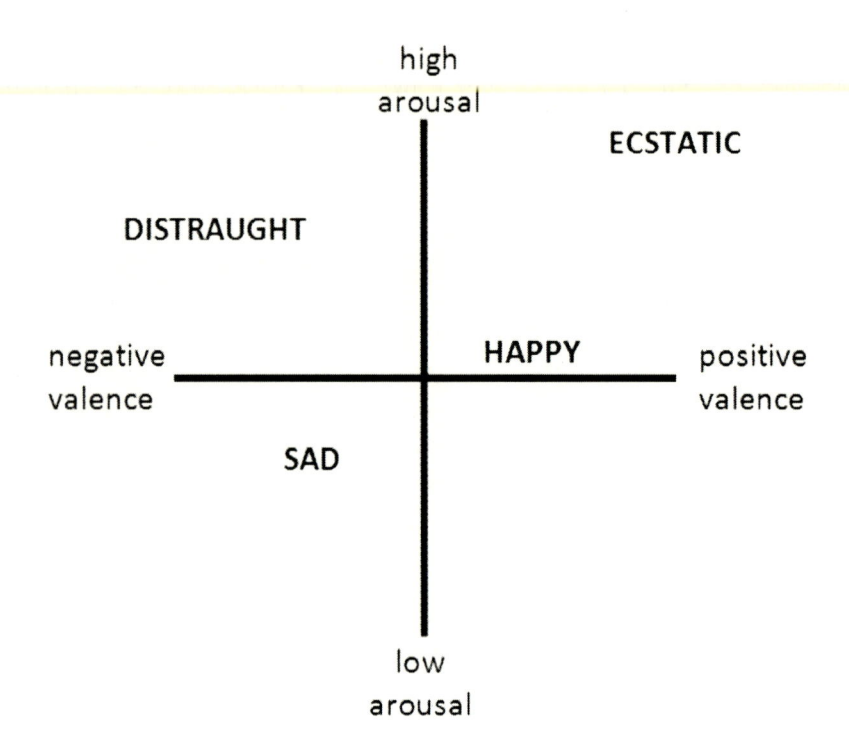

Figure 2.1.

The basic six emotions that exist outside of cultural barriers are believed to be happiness, sadness, fear, disgust, surprise, and anger (Sauter, Eisner, Ekman, & Scott, 2010). As indicated, basic emotions differ in the amount of valence and arousal associated with each one.

What you may now be asking yourself is if there are only six basic emotions, how is it that we experience such a range and assortment of other feelings? The answer is that the "big six" form the basis for all other emotional responses. That is to say that other *secondary* emotions are derived from the primary emotions. For example, the so-called self-conscious secondary emotions of shame, pride, hubris, and regret are all derived from the basic emotion of disgust (Lewis, 1993). Secondary emotions are influenced heavily by social context and the mores associated with a culture.

Though a description of emotions may seem slightly out of place in a chapter on perception, much of the influence of emotion upon cognition has to do with our subjective appraisal or interpretation of a stimulus. For example, an image or the thought of a raw steak may make some of you, presumably the hardcore meat-eaters of the bunch, salivate (it is an appetitive stimulus), whereas vegetarians and vegans would be disgusted (an aversive stimulus).

Differences in emotional perception and the associated responses are critically important to most, if not all, forms of cognition. Indeed, though once upon a time it was believed that the presence of emotional responses inhibited or in some ways impaired cognition, we now know that cognition and emotion must be viewed together. As we will see in the coming chapters, the latter can have enhancing as well as impairing effects upon the former.

Visual sensitivity is measured by determining at what point we cease to see distinct patterns of black and white alternating lines (i.e., sine gratings) and begin to instead see them as one diffuse gray area. This *contrast sensitivity* is a marker of visual acuity and is similar phenomenologically to the loss of visual detail as you move farther away from a picture. As an example of the facilitating effect of emotion on cognition, visual contrast sensitivity has been shown to be enhanced when negative emotional stimuli (frightened faces) are also presented (Phelps, Ling, & Carrasco, 2006). Importantly, the enhancing power of emotion upon perception is not only relegated to the negative emotions, as positive emotions have a similar effect (Zeelenberg, Wagenmakers, & Rotteveel, 2006). Contrary to the notions of emotion-induced "tunnel vision" or the act of "seeing red," we actually see better when there is emotion involved than when there isn't.

Not only does emotion enhance perception but emotions themselves are perceived quite readily. We often wear our emotions on our faces. This outward expression of our internal state is detected quite readily by others. As discussed, there are distinct areas of the brain that are specifically evolved to detect and focus on faces. Furthermore, emotions are actually detected neurologically before other cognitive processes are even activated (Dolan, 2002). Thus our feelings are readily detected by others, even if we don't want them to be.

This all means that how teachers look and sound when talking to students can be quite revealing. Participants were asked to rate teachers' perceptions of the students to whom they were speaking from brief (ten-second) audio and video clips. Though the clips only focused on the teachers' behaviors and did not show the students, participants as young as fourth grade were able to successfully differentiate between two types of students being addressed by the teachers: those who were considered to be "high" achieving and those who were "low" achieving (Babad, Bernieri, & Rosenthal, 1991). The teacher interacted with the "high"-achieving student more positively than with the "low"-achieving student. With less than half a minute of observation, our perceptions of how others, in this case teachers, feel about students can be readily identified.

As the authors readily point out in the discussion of their findings, with only 10 seconds of film footage, there was barely enough time for the teachers to utter more than two words; thus truly it was the manner in which the teachers addressed the students and not the content of their discussion that affected the ratings of how the teacher felt about each student.

Though these findings may seem to speak directly to so-called *expectancy effects*, namely the finding that how students perform in a class may be largely influenced by how the teacher feels about them (Rosenthal & Jacobson, 1968), our focus here is more upon student comfort than academic performance. Now more than four decades after *Pygmalion in the Classroom* thrust the idea of teacher expectancy effects into the professional and public vernaculars (Rosenthal & Jacobson, 1968), there is still a fair amount of controversy regarding just how strongly teacher expectations of students affect student intelligence and performance (Jussim & Harber, 2005).

Rather than wade into those murky waters, we will instead focus on the indisputable points that because detection of emotions is instinctual, teachers must be incredibly careful and conscientious about how they deal with all students in a classroom, particularly those who are "easy" and those who are seen as more "challenging." Given the fact that teacher interactions with students influence how those students are perceived by their peers (Birch & Ladd, 1998), the case for conscious monitoring of behavior cannot be overstated.

It is recommended that educators plan ahead for interactions with students they may consider more trying or challenging than others. Just as the successful teacher plans for contingencies such as having extra supplies for students who may forget or be unable to afford their own, so must she also plan ahead for the possibility of questions, to which an-

PERCEPTION OF TIME

Why is it that time flies when one is having fun, and is this truly the case? The perception of time is an interesting phenomenon because in the short-term, it doesn't directly relate to any of our senses per se. Though daylight attunes our bodies to cyclic 24-hour (roughly) rhythms based on the specialized neurons in our retina that connect to a portion of the hypothalamus called the suprachiasmatic nucleus (SCN; Dibner, Schibler, & Albrecht, 2010), our perception of how much time has passed in minutes and hours is not linked to any direct sensory input. Because there is no true reference point, such as the sun, our perception of time is susceptible to manipulation by several different factors.

Physical characteristics can affect judgments of duration. A well-known mediator of our perception of how long something lasts is whether it was presented as a sound or an image (Goldstone, Boardman, & Lhamon, 1959; Wearden, Todd, & Jones, 2006). Even when the same information is presented for the same amount of time, the audio information is perceived as lasting longer than the visual. This virtual stretching of time for sounds should be remembered when presenting information to students. That is, there may be circumstances or activities in which it is beneficial to actually read a list to students rather than rely on a PowerPoint, overhead transparencies, or some other visual medium.

The size of stimuli that are presented also affects our perception of how long we feel that they were presented (Xuan et al., 2007). Put differently, large arrays of information are perceived as lasting longer than smaller arrays of information. Findings such as these suggest that the brain may use similar, if not the same, neurological and cognitive processes to assess magnitude and quantity, regardless of if the information relates to questions of quantity, spatial relationships, or time (Walsh, 2003). Findings such as these suggest that those students who have problems with mathematics and comparative number sense may also have issues with time management, perhaps due to less-than-optimal processing in the right inferior parietal cortex (Walsh, 2003).

In addition, the fact that experiencing awe causes people to feel as though they have more time available to them than they in fact may have is further proof that there is a common mechanism underlying our sense of magnitude (Rudd, Vohs, & Aaker, 2012). By definition, awe is a positive emotion that imbues an individual with a sense of things that are vast and limitless (Keltner & Haidt, 2003). By having individuals either watch an awe-inducing video (featuring images of waterfalls, space, etc.) or writing about a time that they felt awe, researchers were able to demonstrate that to those individuals time seemed less pressing and they experienced fewer feelings of impatience than individuals who watched videos that made them feel happy or recalled a happy time in their lives (Rudd, Vohs, & Aaker, 2012).

In a classroom setting, many students can feel stressed about exams or class projects because they feel as though they may not have enough time. Perhaps by inducing a sense of awe in these students, the successful teacher can allay some of the perceptions of a time "crunch." Though this particular connection is admittedly one without further empirical support, it is intriguing to consider. Furthermore, because awe is a positive emotion, even if it doesn't help assuage undue test anxiety, it will at least brighten a student's day for a moment.

How does one evoke awe? Images of natural splendor or beauty, moving musical passages, or brief anecdotes about the successful exploits of famous individuals may all achieve this goal.

Effort actually influences our sense of how soon or far off something feels. Tasks and events that are believed to require effort and be taxing actually feel as though they are temporally closer than easier tasks. This only holds true if there is an actual deadline for completion. With a deadline or due date/time in place, it feels as though there is more time to complete the easy task and less time to complete the challenging one (Jiga-Boy, Clark, & Semin, 2010). Without a deadline, more effortful tasks seem farther away in time than they actually are.

These findings suggest that ambiguous or vague deadlines may actually result in greater levels of procrastination because to the student it feels as though there is more time to complete the project than perhaps is actually warranted. Thus it is recommended that firm deadlines be implemented and adhered to whenever possible.

Finally, time does indeed appear to fly when people are having fun (Gable & Poole, 2012). This fact provides yet another reason (as though any were needed) to introduce as much fun and frivolity as possible into classroom sessions because if hard-to-reach students feel as though the day is speeding by, there is less of a chance of them associating the school day with tedium and toil. After all, a happy student is likely an engaged one.

PERCEPTION IN CONTEXT: THE ROLE OF CULTURE

Even with the so-called "flattening" of the world (Friedman, 2006), there are still cultural differences that define and differentiate one group of people from another. For researchers, differences between individuals from East Asia (usually Japan or China) and the West (primarily the United States) provide sufficient differences to examine the influence of culture upon cognition.

Cultural differences

The Asian cultures that are studied are often generalized as being more holistic than Western nations, where there is a focus on individualism. These cultural differences have been found to relate to how scenes and even emotions are perceived. When viewing pictures of complex scenes, the eyes of Chinese participants focus more on the background and on peripheral objects than the eyes of American participants, who primarily look at the primary objects or those items in the foreground (Chua, Boland, & Nisbett, 2005).

These unconscious, culturally defined behaviors, in turn, translate into cultural differences. In general, East Asians are more attuned to changes to background context and the relationships between objects than Americans, who are more adept at detecting modifications to individual objects or subjects (Nisbett & Miyamoto, 2005).

As a whole, American society is seen as being more emotional than that of Japan. Consistent with this generalization, Japanese participants seem to infer emotional states using more information from the eyes, which convey less information, than American participants who rely more heavily upon the shape of the mouth, which is more malleable and displays a wider variety of emotion (Masuda et al., 2008).

On the surface, it may seem that the studies described are only of use to educators who have students from both Eastern and Western cultures in the same room. More than providing the reader with specific evidence-based solutions for accommodating cultural differences in instruction and assessment, these examples are provided to illustrate the degree to which culture can influence unconscious cognitive processes.

It bears mentioning that cultural differences have nothing to do with intelligence or aptitude. It is hoped that the cognitively savvy educator will appreciate the unique perspectives—literally—that students from various backgrounds may have and exploit those differences to optimize and expand the learning opportunities for all students in a classroom.

CONCLUSION

The goal of this chapter, the first to examine a cognitive process, was to provide a broad examination of the ways in which our experience of visual, auditory, emotional, and temporal information can actually differ from reality. It is important to recognize that perception is a reconstructive process, not a duplicative one. Once armed with the understanding that students are drawn to our faces and eyes and that they unconsciously interpret and modify sensory information, educators can be aware of their own practices and behaviors that may enhance, or inhibit, student learning.

POINTS TO REMEMBER

- The sights and sounds that we experience are not the same sights and sounds that were detected by our eyes and ears.
- The brain uses our knowledge and past experiences when interpreting information from our senses, which may result in perceptual inaccuracies.
- Because we use the same brain regions to interpret signals from our eyes and to imagine objects using our mind's eye, it is difficult to do both simultaneously. The same holds true for our sense of hearing and our ability to imagine sounds.
- Many animals, including humans, have specialized neurons in sensory and motor regions of the brain that become activated when we see someone engage in an action. Researchers are beginning to learn how important these mirror neurons are for many forms of cognition.
- Humans have a specialized area of the brain that is responsible for perceiving faces.
- Maintaining eye contact is important for social reasons and has been linked to better student learning.
- Emotions are short-lived affective responses to stimuli, which are comprised of two components: arousal and valence. Arousal has to do with the level of excitement experienced and valence has to do with how pleasant one feels.
- Whereas some emotions are universally human, others are influenced by culture.
- Emotion enhances visual sensitivity.
- Emotions can be detected rapidly and without words. Student perceptions of how teachers and others feel about them can impact their learning.
- Auditory information appears to last longer than visual information, even when the two are presented for the same amount of time.
- Because the brain may use the same areas to judge spatial and temporal magnitude (i.e., how large something is or how much time something will take), students who struggle with mathematics may also have time management issues.
- Positive and negative emotions can influence how we perceive time. Stress can cause time to feel "crunched" and happiness does, in fact, cause time to "fly."

REFERENCES

Babad, E., Bernieri, F., & Rosenthal, R. (1991). Students as judges of teachers' verbal and nonverbal behavior. *American Educational Research Journal, 28*(1), 211–234.

Birch, S. H., & Ladd, G. W. (1998). Children's interpersonal behaviors and the teacher–child relationship. *Developmental Psychology, 34*(5), 934.

Chua, H. F., Boland, J. E., & Nisbett, R. E. (2005). Cultural variation in eye movements during scene perception. *Proceedings of the National Academy of Sciences of the United States of America, 102*(35), 12629–12633.

Dibner, C., Schibler, U., & Albrecht, U. (2010). The mammalian circadian timing system: Organization and coordination of central and peripheral clocks. *Annual Review of Physiology, 72*, 517–549.

Dolan, R. J. (2002). Emotion, cognition, and behavior. *Science, 298*(5596), 1191–1194.

Friedman, T. L. (2006). *The world is flat [updated and expanded]: A brief history of the twenty-first century*. Farrar, Straus and Giroux.

Frischen, A., Bayliss, A. P., & Tipper, S. P. (2007). Gaze cueing of attention: Visual attention, social cognition, and individual differences. *Psychological Bulletin, 133*(4), 694.

Gable, P. A., & Poole, B. D. (2012). Time flies when you're having approach-motivated fun: Effects of motivational intensity on time perception. *Psychological Science, 23*(8), 879–886.

Ganis, G., Thompson, W. L., & Kosslyn, S. M. (2004). Brain areas underlying visual mental imagery and visual perception: An fMRI study. *Cognitive Brain Research, 20*(2), 226–241.

Goldstone, S., Boardman, W. K., & Lhamon, W. T. (1959). Intersensory comparisons of temporal judgments. *Journal of Experimental Psychology, 57*, 243–248.

Goswami, U. (2006). Neuroscience and education: from research to practice? *Nature Reviews Neuroscience, 7*(5), 406-411.

Jiga-Boy, G. M., Clark, A. E., & Semin, G. R. (2010). So much to do and so little time: Effort and perceived temporal distance. *Psychological Science, 21*(12), 1811–1817.

Jussim, L., & Harber, K. D. (2005). Teacher expectations and self-fulfilling prophecies: Knowns and unknowns, resolved and unresolved controversies. *Personality and Social Psychology Review, 9*(2), 131–155.

Kanwisher, N., McDermott, J., & Chun, M. M. (1997). The fusiform face area: A module in human extrastriate cortex specialized for face perception. *The Journal of Neuroscience, 17*(11), 4302–4311.

Kanwisher, N. (2010). Functional specificity in the human brain: A window into the functional architecture of the mind. *Proceedings of the National Academy of Sciences, 107*(25), 11163–11170.

Kelley, D. H., & Gorham, J. (1988). Effects of immediacy on recall of information. *Communication Education, 37*(3), 198–207.

Keltner, D., & Haidt, J. (2003). Approaching awe, a moral, spiritual, and aesthetic emotion. *Cognition and Emotion, 17*, 297–314.

Lewis, M. (1993). The emergence of human emotions. *Handbook of Emotions, 2*, 253–322.

Marzano, R. J., Frontier, T., & Livingston, D. (2011). *Effective supervision: Supporting the art and science of teaching. Association for Supervision & Curriculum Development*. Association for Supervision & Curriculum Development: Arlington, VA.

Masuda, T., Ellsworth, P. C., Mesquita, B., Leu, J., Tanida, S., & van de Veerdonk, E. (2008). Placing the face in context: Cultural differences in the perception of facial emotion. *Journal of Personality and Social Psychology, 94*, 365–381.

McCroskey, J. C., Sallinen, A., Fayer, J. M., Richmond, V. P., & Barraclough, R. A. (1996). Nonverbal immediacy and cognitive learning: A cross-cultural investigation. *Communication Education, 45*(3), 200–211.

Mehrabian, A. (1968). Some referents and measures of nonverbal behavior. *Behavior Research Methods, 1*(6), 203–207.

Nisbett, R. E., & Miyamoto, Y. (2005). The influence of culture: Holistic versus analytic perception. *Trends in Cognitive Sciences, 9*(10), 467–473.

Phelps, E. A., Ling, S., & Carrasco, M. (2006). Emotion facilitates perception and potentiates the perceptual benefit of attention. *Psychological Science, 17*, 292–299.

Rafaeli, E., & Revelle, W. (2006). A premature consensus: Are happiness and sadness truly opposite affects? *Motivation and Emotion, 30*(1), 1–12.

Rekart, J. L., Rekart, K. N., and Bizeur, J. (2008). *Affective ratings of words provide support for multiple arousal dimensions.* Association for Psychological Science, Chicago, IL, II-002.

Rizzolatti, G., & Sinigaglia, C. (2010). The functional role of the parieto-frontal mirror circuit: Interpretations and misinterpretations. *Nature Reviews Neuroscience, 11*(4), 264–274.

Rosenthal, R., & Jacobson, L. (1968). *Pygmalion in the classroom: Teacher expectation and pupils' intellectual development.* Holt, Rinehart & Winston.

Rudd, M., Vohs, K. D., & Aaker, J. (2012). Awe expands people's perception of time, alters decision making, and enhances well-being. *Psychological Science, 23,* 1130–1136.

Sauter, D. A., Eisner, F., Ekman, P., & Scott, S. K. (2010). Cross-cultural recognition of basic emotions through nonverbal emotional vocalizations. *Proceedings of the National Academy of Sciences, 107*(6), 2408–2412.

Senju, A., & Johnson, M. H. (2009). Atypical eye contact in autism: Models, mechanisms and development. *Neuroscience & Biobehavioral Reviews, 33*(8), 1204–1214.

Shepard, R. N., & Metzler, J. (1971). Mental rotation of three-dimensional objects. *Science, 171,* 701–703.

Walsh V. (2003). A theory of magnitude: Common cortical metrics of time, space and quantity. *Trends in Cognitive Sciences, 7,* 483–488.

Wearden, J. H., Todd, N. P. M., & Jones, L. A. (2006). When do auditory/visual differences in duration judgments occur? *The Quarterly Journal of Experimental Psychology, 59*(10), 1709–1724.

Witt, P. L., Wheeless, L. R., & Allen, M. (2006). The relationship between teacher immediacy and student learning: A meta-analysis. Classroom communication and instructional processes: Advances through meta-analysis, In Gayle, B. M., Preiss, R. W., Burrell, N., and Allen, M. *Classroom Communication and instructional processes: Advances through meta-analysis* (149–160). Mahwah, NJ. Lawrence Earlbaum Associates Publishers.

Xuan, B., Zhang, D., He, S., & Chen, X. (2007). Larger stimuli are judged to last longer. *Journal of Vision, 7*(10).

Zeelenberg, R., Wagenmakers, E. J., & Rotteveel, M. (2006). The impact of emotion on perception bias or enhanced processing? *Psychological Science, 17*(4), 287–291.

THREE
Attention

"You'll never learn anything if you don't pay attention." This seemingly sage advice is echoed by teachers (and parents) everywhere. Though not entirely accurate (*latent* learning does occur in the absence of attention), there is enough truth to the statement that we should ask questions about how exactly it is that attention facilitates learning. Why is it so important to pay (such an odd verb choice, really; to whom is payment made) attention?

For the cognitive psychologist, attention refers to the act of dedicating conscious, cognitive resources to a set of stimuli. Roughly translated, this merely means to direct one's mind toward one or more things (Anderson, 1995). Both the terms "focus" and "concentration" refer to varying levels of attention, with the latter connoting a more single-minded dedication of the mind than the former.

THE NATURE OF ATTENTION

When we direct our mind (or focus or concentrate) toward a task, problem, or line of thought, what we are really doing is readying various cognitive processes that may be used. If we focus our attention upon the problem "D+C=____," we prepare our mind to run through our memory stores for a clue as to what this might mean, we engage processes that will enable us to learn what this is so that we may recall it at a later time, and we actively initiate problem-solving centers of the brain to start applying algorithms and heuristics.

Instructions for where to direct our attention can come from inside or outside of us. When a fire alarm sounds in a building, it immediately becomes the "center" of our attention. This external stimulus demands our attention. Why is this? It is because the salient physical features of the alarm, in this case volume and the tone, "grab" our attention in such a way that we don't have any choice but to acknowledge and become aware of its existence.

The fact that external stimuli can dictate "what" we attend to follows from early studies conducted by Broadbent (1958) and others (c.f. Lachter, Forster, and Ruthruff, 2004) and is something intuitively used by individuals when they whistle or talk loudly to gain attention in a crowded room.

External stimuli don't have to be loud (or bright or stinky) to be noticed. Other features of stimuli can also grab and direct our attention. Information that is personally relevant will sometimes, though not always (Treisman, 1969), redirect our attention.

For example, imagine you are at a crowded party and are actively engaged in a conversation with a few other party-goers. As often happens at large gatherings, small clusters of people will form, with each cluster engaged in a unique topic of conversation. The only way for anyone in one of the smaller clusters to follow the conversation for that particular group is to direct attention toward the voice(s) that are closest and ignore all of the others. Despite the fact that you are ignoring all of the other voices/conversations going on, if someone outside of your immediate conversation were to say your name, you might actually hear it, even though you failed to hear anything else that was said. If this were to occur, then you would experience what is known as the "cocktail party" effect (Cherry, 1953). Because our own names are important to us and have relevance, they grab our attention.

Alternatively, you can also be so engaged in your own conversation that you miss everything else around you, even if you're the subject of discussion. Or perhaps you weren't listening to what was being said even in your own small group. Instead, you "zoned out" in the middle, focused on your internal mind's voice, and ceased to hear whatever the speaker was saying. In those cases, the shift of attention internally leaves little left for you to devote to listening to what occurs externally (i.e., the fellow party-goer's voice).

Indeed, our inability to simultaneously think deeply about something and listen fully to someone talk is illustrative of the limitations of our attentional systems. If attention is something which truly must be "paid," then let's examine what the cognitive "accounting" looks like. In this case, we need to note that the total amount of attention that we can devote is limited and largely fixed. Thus if we choose to devote the bulk of our attention to one task, there is very little "left over" for other tasks.

Capacity theories (e.g., Kahneman) often use the analogy of attention as a pie (rather than as a bank account with fixed limits and a strict non-overdraft policy). Because both internal and external stimuli compete for the same attentional pie, if one piece gets larger (e.g., worries about an ongoing snowstorm outside), there is less "pie" to divide among whatever else requires attention (e.g., the lively party discourse).

Though a number of brain regions are involved in attention, two that are central to attention are the prefrontal cortex and anterior cingulate cortex (Sturm & Willmes, 2001). These areas help to plan our actions, including upon what and where we will focus our attention at a given moment. Both of these regions have been implicated in decision making and planning (e.g., what to wear to a party in two weeks) in general (Cohen, Botvinick, & Carter, 2000), suggesting the similarities involved in deciding where to consciously direct attention and how to direct one's life in the long term.

These same two regions also "mature" more slowly than other brain regions and have not reached full potential even in late adolescence (Eshel, Nelson, Blair, Pine, & Emst, 2007). Thus challenges with getting teenagers (or younger children) to focus or to think about the long-term ramifications of their actions likely stem from the same developmental "lag" in brain maturation. In contrast, areas responsible for directing attention to external stimuli (e.g., a loud "bang" that grabs our attention), such as the pulvinar nucleus of the thalamus and the superior colliculus (Posner, Cohen, & Rafal, 1982), reach adult levels of functionality relatively early in development (Johnson, 2002).

COGNITIVE LOAD AND THE ATTENTIONAL PIE

Though the overall amount of attention that is available at any one time is limited, the demands upon attention, those slices of our attentional pie, are not all the same size nor do they remain the same size. Many factors influence the size of the slices (i.e., demands), including cue salience, motivation, emotions, and practice. When we consciously decide to focus our attention on a given task, we increase the size of that slice relative to the other demands that could be processed, which leaves less total attention for other demands.

Learning how to read is one of the most challenging endeavors that a child will encounter. Part of the challenge lies in the fact that orthographic symbols (letters and words) represent actual sounds (phonemes) which are themselves symbols that represent the actual concepts and thoughts that are to be conveyed (see chapter 8 for more on language).

When elementary school students are learning to read, it is an effortful process that requires a great deal of focus and attention. Sounding out some words ("f-i-s-h"), recognizing others that don't have nice 1:1 letter to sound correspondence ("w-h-a-l-e"), and making sense of what all of the words mean together is a complicated, cognitive, resource-draining exercise. However, once we've mastered something like reading, it begins to require seemingly no effort at all. Once mastered, we can read while we are engaged in other tasks because of the freeing of attentional resources that takes place with automaticity.

For example, imagine you are driving to a friend's house which you've never previously visited (pretend there isn't any GPS). While engaged in all of the activities related to driving (e.g., scanning the road, checking your mirrors, changing the radio station), you also have to sound out every street name, restaurant and business sign, and so forth. In this scenario, the amount of attention required to read all of the signage along your path would seriously distract you from the road. Despite this, the vast majority of licensed drivers (i.e., those 16 years of age or older) don't have any such difficulties. So, why the differences in attentional resources required to read (and drive as well) between the beginning reader and expert driver? The answer is a simple one: practice.

Over time, the amount of effort required for some behaviors becomes easier and easier. This is the case for many day-to-day activities that we now take for granted, such as driving, using a fork, typing, and reading. Despite all of the challenges involved in reading, after years of practice, it becomes an *automatic* process. The automaticity of reading is helpful because it frees up attentional resources to meet other demands (Schneider & Chein, 2003). Indeed, most activities that we do simultaneously, like reading street signs while driving, are made possible only because of automatic processes.

To demonstrate how automaticity works, we'll engage in a brief bit of mathematics. The key to the following exercise is to come up with the answer *in your head* as quickly as possible before checking your answer using a pen and paper or a calculator, if needed. Ready? Solve the following problem:

$$6 \times 9 = \underline{\qquad}?$$

Did you get the correct answer? Chances are excellent that you did get the correct answer and likely in no time flat. Let's try another:

$$16 \times 19 = \underline{\qquad}?$$

How about now? Likely this second question took you longer. Even once you had solved it, you may not have been confident in your answer the way you were for the first problem. The difference between the two sets of problems is that the former is one that most of us learned in second or third grade, probably using a drill method where we memorized all of the products of 6 from 1 to 9 (e.g., 6×5, 6×6, etc.).

We may have been graded, when first learning these "times tables," for both accuracy and speed. Rewards for individuals and/or the class may have been used to motivate retention (my second grade teacher offered my class a microwave popcorn party when we all made our way through the 1 through 9 times tables—talk about high stakes testing!). The point is that 6 x 9 was something that we practiced, practiced, and practiced again until we got it. Now that it has been mastered, we continue to reap the rewards of our early efforts today. When confronted with the question, all that needs to happen is for us to recall the answer from memory (Logan, 1988), which requires decidedly less effort than the calculation.

The product of 16 x 19, however, is not one that most of us had to memorize (and if we didn't *have* to memorize it, chances are good that we didn't do so on our own). Thus to come up with the answer of 304, we can't just grab the answer from memory but have to actually engage in multiplying the numbers together, carrying numbers, and then adding together the two levels—all of which requires effort. Though we can see how automaticity can have its benefits, there are times when automaticity can actually interfere with other processes.

When participants are presented with lists of words that are different colors, they have little trouble identifying the color of each word as long as the color of the word and the word itself match (e.g., the word "BLUE" that is presented in blue ink). Interestingly, if the word and the color it is printed in are different (e.g., the word "BLUE" printed in red ink), people have difficulties naming the color of the word.

This well-known phenomenon, called the Stroop effect (1935), occurs because for adults reading is an automatic process. Thus even though the task is to name colors—something people have been doing for decades with ease—the reading of the words occurs without conscious instruction and interferes with the completion of the task. Though automatic processes are helpful because they reduce the amount of cognitive resources required to complete the task, automaticity comes at a price. When we have to actually use resources and effort to inhibit the process (as is necessary with the mismatched word colors and words), the automaticity of the process can hinder our completion of other tasks.

Practice can actually reduce the amount of mental effort required to complete a task (unless we have to actually inhibit the automatic process itself) such as reading. The automaticity of reading does break down, however, when words that aren't neutral, such as colors, are used. Everyday language has a great deal of ambiguity built into it. For example, the statement "What do you think about those apples?" can be a perfectly simple question about whether somebody enjoyed the taste of a nice red Macoun or Fuji apple. On the other hand, it could be a rhetorical question used to taunt somebody who is getting his comeuppance.

Our interpretation of the exact meaning relies on context, emotional states (our own and that of the speaker), and other factors. The act of determining the true meaning behind words and statements can make an automatic process like reading into an effortful one.

Though many teenagers (and some adults) don't realize it, one of the reasons why texting while driving is so incredibly dangerous has to do with the ambiguity of text speak and our need to get at exactly what somebody was trying to communicate to us in fewer than 200 characters. Using a simulated driving task, researchers at the University of Utah demonstrated that the amount of time it takes to effectively brake is increased by 69 percent when someone reads a text relative to the amount of time it takes when not texting. In contrast, an increase of *only* 34 percent relative to non-texters was observed when drivers sent a text (Drews, Yazdani, Godfrey, Cooper, & Strayer, 2009).

In some ways, this finding is counterintuitive as sending a text requires our hands (or at least thumbs) and eyes, but reading only requires the latter. The difference between these two texting behaviors is likely due, in part, to the fact that our brain tries to makes sense of not only the text itself but also the emotion that the text is meant to convey (see chapter 7 for more on texting).

WHEN THE BRAIN DECIDES IT IS TIME TO FOCUS ELSEWHERE

Sometimes our brains decide to stop paying attention even though it may not be in our best interest. This disengagement, which is referred to as an *attentional blink*, occurs subconsciously when our brains believe that a task has been completed. As the term suggests, an attentional blink is a short period (approximately half a second) during which incoming information is not registered—similar to what happens to visual information during the blink of an eye (Shapiro, Raymond, & Arnell, 1997).

This phenomenon, which is quite robust, is most often studied by presenting a series of letters, numbers, or other stimuli rapidly to participants (called a *rapid serial visual presentation* task or RSVP). Two of the stimuli that are presented are targets (T1 and T2), which are to be recognized by the participant. If after the first target (T1) is found, the second (T2) is not, then an attentional blink has occurred.

An attentional blink occurs because of a disengagement from attention rather than a lack of perception. Thus it is not that visual information isn't *seen* per se but rather that it isn't perceived (Vogel & Luck, 2002). A diffuse network of brain regions work together, including the occipital, temporal, parietal, and frontal lobes (Hommel et al., 2006), to free cognitive resources once the first target is seen, thus even though the second target is presented and seen, the brain centers responsible for recognizing the target are not activated and the second target goes by unnoticed.

Though it may seem as though there are few, if any, situations in a classroom in which visual stimuli are presented in such rapid succession, like the RSVP task, that an attentional disengagement could be a factor, attentional blinks may, in fact, occur. Let's look at a sample question (from a class on classic movies, perhaps?) that utilizes a well-known multiple choice format.

Which of the following is a character from *Star Wars, Episode IV*?

a) Han Solo
b) Greedo
c) Snaggletooth
d) All of the above

As any fan of the 1977 classic knows, all three of the characters listed were in the film. However, when tests are structured in this manner, it is possible after a student reads the first option (Han Solo) and recognizes it as correct, that an attentional blink could occur. The blink prevents the student from considering, or perhaps even being aware of, any of the other options. Because in this case the other options (Greedo and Snaggletooth) are also correct, the last option (which is farthest away from the recognized "target" in this scenario) is actually the only correct answer.

Though this was certainly a low-stakes test, in actual classroom settings, there is a great deal of pressure associated with examinations. Indeed, all tests can provoke some form of anxiety, standardized or not. It is known that anxiety likely increases the attentional blink (MacLean and Arnell, 2010), thus it is unfortunate that multiple choice tests structured in this manner (with the possibility that both the first and last answer could both be technically correct) could impair performance as a result of an unconscious (and possibly uncontrollable) cognitive phenomenon.

Luckily, there is an easy remedy for minimizing the possibility of attentional blinks masking true knowledge on a multiple-choice test. Rather than using the last option to test whether students recognize that multiple items are all correct (i.e., options "a" through "c"), simply move the option from "d" to "a" and revise accordingly. Thus the sample question from before becomes:

Which of the following is a character from *Star Wars, Episode IV*?

a) All of the following are characters
b) Han Solo
c) Greedo
d) Snaggletooth

With the response items structured in this way, the student is notified right away that there is a possibility that each of the options could be correct. Though this may seem relatively picayune, minor modifications to assessments such as these may be particularly important as studies have found that the impulsivity is a predictor of the likelihood of attentional blinks occurring (Ray Li et al., 2005). Thus attentional blinks may be most problematic for those students who are the most impulsive (which, with teenagers, is on a sliding scale).

TECHNOLOGY AND ATTENTION

A colleague of mine, who is an expert on special education, commented that technology is creating a "culture of ADHD (attention-deficit/hyperactivity disorder)." Though not personally willing to commit to such a dire pronouncement, I am concerned about how the routine usage of technology *is* affecting our capacity for sustained and focused attention.

While the widespread proliferation of computers has made it easier for students to *complete* homework, projects, and research reports, in some cases technology may actually impede the *learning* that it is supposed to facilitate. *Media multitasking* is used to describe the modern-day phenomenon of using multiple electronic devices or multiple programs within one device to seemingly do multiple things simultaneously.

An example of media multitasking that is likely occurring across Western countries right now involves a student texting on her phone while working on a paper (i.e., school work) that is open on a laptop while updating her status and reading updates from others on Facebook and listening to music on an iPod. The television may even be on as well.

When our hypothetical student attempts to do several things at the same time, as occurs with media multitasking, her attention is divided. As we know from our earlier discussion of attentional pie, as the number of demands from each of the media (i.e., text message, status updates from Facebook) increases, the amount of attention that can be paid to any one task decreases. What is problematic is that when there are multiple, non-automatic processes that are occurring concurrently, the brain lacks the necessary resources to complete any of the tasks the way it would if they were being done in isolation.

So how prevalent is media multitasking? Using student diaries and survey data, Foehr found that 58 percent of seventh through twelfth graders multitask other media while reading "most" or "some" of the time, while 64 percent report doing "multiple things at the same time on the computer" (2006). This figure is similar to what was seen when college student multitasking behavior online was assessed using an experience sampling approach (multitasking occurred 57 percent of the time; Moreno et al., 2012).

Unlike members of other generations, members of the Net generation feel comfortable and efficacious when multitasking (Carrier et al., 2009). Comfort can be misleading, however, as our biases can cloud our ability to see: (1) how much time we spend performing a particular behavior and (2) the negative impact of those behaviors. For example, college-aged students and college staff were seated in a laboratory with an HDTV and a laptop and told they may do whatever they liked with either or both devices for a half an hour. The behaviors, including the amount of time they gazed at either device, were video recorded and analyzed. When asked how often they thought they would switch between a simultaneously presented television program and a computer screen, the participants estimated they would switch about 15 times during the half-hour session. Participants' estimates were off by a long shot as it was found that, in fact, on average participants switched between the two media 123 times; a difference of over 8-fold (Brasel & Gips, 2011).

The aforementioned study reinforces the fact that we are poor judges of how much we use and interact with electronic devices. If we were better at assessing our own usage, then we would either know that we are likely to switch back and forth every 12 seconds or we would realistically only do so every 2 minutes, which is the frequency predicted by a total of 15 switches.

The media multitasking deficit that was described is even seen when there is too much information presented simultaneously, even if the information is all presented from the same media source. One prime example of this may be found on any modern cable news program. At the bottom of the screen of major news outlets is the news "crawl," the continuous, right-to-left banner of words that reports on sports updates, celebrity weddings, and world events. This crawl is present even when reporters report and pundits pontificate. What's more, information presented by the two (the main report and the crawl) don't even have to be related, and most of the time are not.

As it turns out, there is a cost to presenting so much information simultaneously, as individuals who watch a standard news program retain approximately 10 percent less information than individuals who watch only the main newscast (with the crawl removed from the viewer's screen; Bergen, Grimes, & Potter, 2005). Even though the latter set of studies was conducted in a controlled laboratory setting, it appears to be fairly robust. First, the researchers explicitly told the participants that they would be tested on the topics presented in the newscast. Second, participants in both conditions were told that they would have to return and re-take the test if they did poorly (thus an attempt to motivate participants to pay exclusive attention to the newscast). Given these two considerations, the most parsimonious explanation is that the news crawl is a distraction. The whole idea that today's "digital natives" are able to seamlessly absorb and integrate information from multiple sources simultaneously is also challenged by these findings, as all of the participants were undergraduate students.

Why does splitting attention decrease retention? Possibly because there are differences in the amount of brain activation observed when two tasks are attempted simultaneously. In a study examining how the brain responds when people multitask, participants were asked to determine whether two objects were the same (i.e., the Shepard and Metzler mental rotation task discussed in chapter 2) while answering questions about geography.

It turns out that the total amount of activity seen when the two were done concurrently was strikingly less than the sum of brain activations that occurred when each task was completed by itself (Just, Carpenter, Keller, Emery, Zajac, & Thulborn, 2001; Newman, Keller, & Just, 2007). Put differently, multitasking decreases the amount of mental resources that can be devoted to any one task.

Reductions in brain activation that are seen with multitasking are related to impairments in learning. In practice, this means that our multitasking student may be able to satisfactorily complete an assignment, and perhaps even get an "A." However, her overall long-term retention and ability to use the information from the assignment is likely to be diminished relative to if she were to complete just the assignment and then engage in social and other media.

Furthermore, not all brain regions are created equally. This is because some are responsible for rote or more simplistic learning whereas the involvement of others is necessary for deep learning. Not only does dividing attention cause a reduction in total brain activation, it may also "recruit" those brain regions that are responsible for habit learning (i.e., the striatum) and not those regions, such as the hippocampus, that underlie true, meaningful learning (Foerde, Knowlton, and Poldrask 2006).

The implications of involving the wrong brain regions are that the type of flexible learning necessary for any of the upper levels of Bloom's taxonomy (Bloom, 1956) aren't facilitated by areas such as the striatum, which are involved in automatic habits. Unfortunately, the benefits of automaticity, discussed earlier, do not seem to matter when it comes to media multitasking (Lin, Robertson, & Lee, 2009).

So, dividing attention away from school has an effect on long-term learning. But are attention spans actually *shorter*? An examination of the ability to switch between concurrent tasks was examined in individuals considered "light" and "heavy" media multitaskers (Ophir, Nass, & Wagner, 2009). It was found that individuals who multitasked more often (i.e., "heavy" media multitaskers) had shorter attention spans than those who did so less often. Attention span length in this study was determined by how easily individuals were distracted by stimuli that weren't related to task completion.

A critical finding of this study was the fact that student habits related to surfing the net, texting, and so forth at home may have direct effects on the ways that information is processed in the classroom. To this end, it has been shown that students who spend more time instant messaging are less likely to read and report being more easily distracted while reading than students who instant message less (Levine, Waite, & Bowman, 2007).

So, the aforementioned findings all speak to the fact that attempting to attend to multiple sources of information has deleterious effects on learning and memory, but are there any ramifications of living in an environment where such behaviors are the norm? Indeed, frequent media multitasking may be affecting one's ability to switch focus between tasks that are important (e.g., a teacher's lecture) and those that may not be (e.g., extraneous sounds in a classroom; Ophir, Nass, & Wagner, 2009).

These results may have far-reaching ramifications as they suggest that lifestyle choices (i.e., media multitasking) may be changing the way an entire generation attends to information.

What happens when everything one encounters has an equal chance of grabbing attention? One possibility is that even irrelevant stimuli, which should be dismissed as unimportant, will grab the attention of students used to responding to random clicks, pop-up windows, and ring tones. An increase in student distractibility presents a challenge for the lecturing teacher trying to maintain the focus of students. In addition, it is problematic for the student taking a test whose focus should be on the examination.

Teachers everywhere will openly lament shrinking "attention spans" and a lack of focus on the part of their students. Professional educators are well aware that an inability to pay attention will limit the amount and quality of learning that can take place. So, given changes in attentional control and the reliance on "study" habits that utilize brain structures that do not facilitate deep learning, what are teachers to do? Fortunately, there are several strategies grounded in sound cognitive scientific research that can be employed to grab and maintain attention. This, in turn, will facilitate learning in the classroom.

In school districts across this country and others, the last decade has seen a major push for what is known as 1:1 computer access. One-to-one initiatives ensure that every student in a school possesses a laptop by providing one for all students (or at least those who don't already own one). Though these programs have been shown to increase student (and teacher) engagement and enhance student technological literacy, there is a dearth of well-designed studies that examine the extent to which such initiatives actually enhance learning and/or contribute to academic success (Zucker & Light, 2009). Given the expense and infrastructure requirements associated with such programs, it is striking that so little is known about the effects of having technology integrated into classroom settings.

On the surface, it seems like common sense that laptops will enhance student learning; however, this does not have to be the case. Though laptops may be seemingly ubiquitous in college and university lecture halls, they may not be having the positive impact that students (and parents) hope they will. In fact, several studies have found that the use of laptops in classrooms (both simulated and real) have negative impacts on academic performance (Hembrooke & Gay, 2003; Fried, 2008; Sana, Weston, & Cepeda, 2013).

Even when students used their laptops exclusively for course-related learning, computer users had lower scores on both multiple choice and short answer–type questions than non-computer users. Perhaps one of the most nefarious findings is that the negative impacts of laptop usage may even be contagious. Individuals in a simulated classroom who were able to directly view others browsing the web and conducting other non-course-related activities actually fared 17 percent worse on examinations of course material than those who were unable to view multitasking classmates (Sana, Weston, & Cepeda, 2013). Thus even others' multitasking habits can distract our attention away from what should be the central focus.

GAINING THE ATTENTION OF TODAY'S STUDENTS

As previously written, the use of laptops in classroom settings *does* enhance student engagement (Zucker & Light, 2009). This is not surprising given that the implementation of a laptop computer into a classroom setting helps to mimic the technologically immersive environment to which most of today's students have grown accustomed. It is easy to see how a classroom is relatively *boring* compared to the actual lives of our students when one considers that they are used to living in a world in which they are continually surprised with new status updates, text messages, instant messages, tweets, emails, animated gifs, crawling news, and videos of piano-playing cats. Furthermore, now that we know that students who are immersed in these environments by choice (i.e., heavy media multitaskers) are actually modifying their cognitive and neurological responses to stimuli (e.g., Ophir, Nass, & Wagner, 2009), it becomes more critical than ever to begin to reexamine the structure of school classrooms.

The first option is to lament the changes that have taken place and put down one's foot. This is the teacher who is so entrenched in traditional learning paradigms and environments that s/he will teach as she was taught and will let the chips, meaning the students' success, fall where they may. An adherence to the *"it worked for me so it will work for them"* philosophy may nurture some self-satisfaction, but it won't change the fact that our world is a technological one and will continue to be so.

The second option is to try and change the students—to somehow help them to adapt to a way of thinking and behaving that is consistent with traditional classroom structures. Though this *may* work within the classroom, it does nothing to prepare students for how to apply and use what they've learned in a traditional setting in one that more closely resembles real life.

The third option entails moving past nostalgia (option one) and working to both get students to embrace the power of focus and concentration (option two) while concomitantly modifying teaching strategies and instructional (and classroom) design to meet the needs of changing minds and brains. It is this third option that is endorsed here.

One way to meet the needs of today's students is to break apart the standard lecture routine. Whereas in secondary (and post-secondary) classrooms, it is commonplace to have an entire class period dedicated to a lecture on one topic, it would be more beneficial to student engagement to distribute instruction over distinct 10-to-12-minute modules rather than have one 50, 60, 75, or even 90-minute period (Rekart, 2011). Often times, we (i.e., those over 30 years of age) fail to remember that we ourselves lost focus in the middle of marathon lectures in high school and college. Indeed, it was the rare teacher or professor who could keep a class rapt with attention for an entire session of lecturing.

By breaking apart the times when information is presented, opportunities are introduced that re-engage students with waning focus. One key way to maintain engagement is to use different instructional vehicles, such as YouTube video clips, pair-share exercises, or debates (Rekart, 2011), for each of the modules. This notion is not a new one, as the benefits of mixing and matching instructional techniques have been advocated by others (e.g., Connell, 2005) and are touted by many as a best practice for general instruction. Where other authors and yours truly may differ, however, is in our rationale for varying the strategies.

The efficacy of the "modular" approach is made possible through the likely activation and recruitment of the brain's medial temporal lobe, including the hippocampus. The hippocampus, which is seen as a novelty detector (e.g., Knight, 1996), becomes activated when something new, such as a new video clip or group activity, is introduced. As discussed earlier, the hippocampus is a brain structure that is critical for the long-term storage and application of learned information. Put differently, it is one of the key parts of the brain, in addition to the frontal cortex, for academic success. Thus the novelty of using multiple instructional methods both engages student attention and is beneficial for long-term learning.

So, if my colleague, quoted earlier, is correct and technology is, in fact, increasing the prevalence of attention-deficit/hyperactivity disorder (ADHD)-like symptoms in the general population, then it stands to reason that techniques used by special educators and some inclusionary teachers will be of benefit to students in general. For example, students with ADHD are easily distracted by unimportant visual and auditory stimuli (Selikowitz, 2009). To remedy the heightened proclivity for distraction, it is recommended that educators reduce the amount of clutter and disorganization of their classrooms. Indeed, by removing extraneous posters, quotes, pictures, and so forth, the classroom teacher can effectively minimize the number of distractions present in the classroom.

The audit of one's classroom is simple: merely ask whether the materials that are present are decorations or truly reinforce learning. If upon reflection one finds that the answer is the former, then the item should be removed.

For example, I can distinctly remember spending what probably amounted to hours over the course of a school year staring at a poster in my third grade classroom. That particular poster had an image of Jedi Master Yoda, from *The Empire Strikes Back*, holding a book and written in red over his head was the word "READ." Though certainly the message of that poster was a good one, its presence in my classroom didn't spur me on to "READ" any more than I already did, but it certainly impaired my ability to "LISTEN" to my teacher, as I daydreamed about the types of books that Yoda would read, wondered how he kept them dry in the swamps of his home planet of Dagobah, and pondered whether he enjoyed the same books that I did. Thus reductions in visual clutter are likely to benefit all students: those with ADHD and without; heavy, light, and non-media multitaskers; and Star Wars nerds and haters.

Whereas reducing visual clutter will positively affect all students, removing auditory distractions will affect students differently depending upon their level of distractibility. Students with ADHD or those who are heavy media multitaskers are used to a higher degree of stimulation than the average classroom provides. Though visual stimuli readily distract the distractible, any ongoing sounds within a classroom may actually prove beneficial to the learning of students with short attention spans. Indeed, Söderlund and colleagues (2010) showed that the learning of students classified as "inattentive" was positively impacted by the inclusion of a low-level white noise generator in a classroom.

On the other hand, the learning of the "attentive" students (i.e., those without any assessed attention deficits) was negatively impacted by the white noise. These findings speak to differences in how auditory information is processed and how easily it can be moved to the "background" in individuals who require more baseline stimulation. In those students who are able to pay attention, it provides an irritating distraction that can actually impair academic success. Thus great care should be taken in modifying the auditory climate of any classroom.

ATTENTION AND CULTURE

Though it can be argued that technology has broadened the cultural chasm between generations—particularly that of so-called Millennials and their grandparents, the Baby Boomers—this form of culture does not constitute the last topic of this chapter. Rather, here we will focus on the influence of geographically instituted cultural differences upon how and what stimuli are attended to by people.

Attention, unlike other cognitive processes, is seldom thought of as being malleable by the environment; however, studies have shown that what and how individuals pay attention to visual stimuli can have decided ramifications for learning and problem solving. The way in which people attend to objects has been studied (developed by Kitayama et al., 2003) using a simple paradigm wherein a vertical line is centered inside of a square (see Figure 3.1).

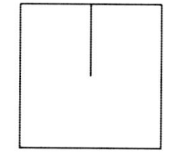

Figure 3.1.

The square and line combination is then followed by another square and line tandem and participants are asked whether the second line resembles the first either (1) absolutely (see option a in the next figure) or (2) relatively (in relation to the square; see option b in the next figure). Note that for the absolute task, the size of the surrounding square shouldn't matter (though it is necessary for the relative task).

a) absolute match   b) relative match

Figure 3.2.

When Americans of Western European ancestry perform these tasks, they do better when making judgments that are absolute rather than relative. Conversely, East Asian participants were better when making relative rather than absolute matches (Kitayama et al., 2003). Based on neurocognitive imaging using fMRI, it has been shown that these two groups perform differently as the result of differences in culturally determined attention.

Whereas Americans from Western European families focus on individuals at the expense of how the individual relates to other items, participants with East Asian backgrounds focus more on the relationship of items to others (i.e., the line to the square). These differences, which are reflective of cultural norms for Western and Eastern societies, speak to the power of external influences on how we view the world (and the stimuli to which we pay attention).

Differences in attentional focus are accompanied by different patterns of brain activation when solving these two tasks (Hedden et al., 2008). Thus culture not only affects the cognitive processes that are readily observed but also the underlying neural circuitry responsible for those behaviors, beliefs, and actions.

Cultural beliefs may be responsible for more than just whether we subconsciously attend more to figures or the ground. Individuals from nations characterized by melancholic brooding are more likely to attend to negative than positive stimuli relative to Americans (Grossman, Ellsworth, & Hong, 2012). As was found with the studies of East Asians and absolute/relative attentional focus, as feelings of national attachment and acculturation increase, so does attention to the culturally associated stimuli.

These findings are mentioned here as it is important for teachers to recognize that the home lives of individual students will impact how and to what they pay attention. Children with a more independent-minded upbringing will be more analytical and are likely to focus on primary concepts with less interest in relationships between concepts and stimuli. On the other hand, those students raised in more collectivistic families or cultures will focus more on how all items, even those in the periphery, relate to one another.

Given that most American teachers will likely fall toward the individualistic end of the spectrum, it is worth mentioning that when students from varying cultural or national backgrounds are integrated into the classroom, efforts will need to be made to both understand their perspectives as well as help them to see things in an individualistic light. It should be noted that neither of these strategies should be considered "best," as each conveys specific benefits upon the user that may prove useful under very different task demands.

POINTS TO REMEMBER

- Attention is the act of directing one's mind toward one or more things.
- Attention may be directed by external or internal stimuli.
- Areas of the brain involved in directing attention are not fully mature until late adolescence.
- There is a limit to the amount of attention that one has. It there is an increase in the focus for one task, this must come at the expense of a decrease in focus for something else.
- When some tasks are mastered, they become automatic, which saves attentional resources. Mastery is achieved through practice and is closely linked to memory.
- Automatic processes can also interfere with cognition if we try to perform a task that we don't normally do.

- Dealing with or interpreting emotional stimuli drains attentional resources, even if we are engaged in an automatic process like reading.
- Attentional blinks occur when our brain stops processing incoming information because it believes that a task has been completed. These may be an issue with student performance on some forms of multiple-choice exams.
- Media multitasking occurs when attention is simultaneously divided among several electronic devices and/or activities, such as phones, email, instant messaging, and texting.
- People underestimate the frequency and duration of their own media multitasking.
- Media multitasking impairs both short- and long-term learning.
- Individuals who media multitask often are more distractible than those who media multitask less. The brains of media multitaskers have been shown to process information differently than non-multitaskers.
- Laptop usage in classrooms may have deleterious effects on attention and learning.
- Breaking up lectures into small modules and decreasing the number of visually distracting stimuli in the physical classroom space may facilitate learning for multitasking youth.
- Culture influences how and to what we pay attention.

REFERENCES

Anderson, J. R. (1995). *Cognitive Psychology and Its Implications*: Fourth Edition. New York: Freeman.

Bergen, L., Grimes, T., & Potter, D. (2005). How attention partitions itself during simultaneous message presentations. *Human Communication Research, 31*(3), 311–336.

Bloom, B. S. (Ed.), Engelhart, M. D., Furst, E. J., Hill, W. H., & Krathwohl, D. R. (1956). *Taxonomy of educational objectives: The classification of educational goals. Handbook 1: Cognitive domain.* New York: David McKay.

Brasel, S. A., & Gips, J. (2011). Media multitasking behavior: Concurrent television and computer usage. *Cyberpsychology, Behavior, and Social Networking, 14*(9), 527–534.

Broadbent, D. E. (1958). *Perception and communication*. New York: Oxford University Press.

Carrier, L. M., Cheever, N. A., Rosen, L. R., Benitez, S., & Chang, J. (2009). Multitasking Across Generations: Multitasking Choices and Difficulty Ratings in Three Generations of Americans. *Computers in Human Behavior, 25*, 483-489.

Cherry, E. C. (1953). Some experiments on the recognition of speech, with one and two ears. *Journal of the Acoustic Society of America, 25*, 975–979.

Cohen, J. D., Botvinick, M., & Carter, C. S. (2000). Anterior cingulate and prefrontal cortex: Who's in control? *Nature Neuroscience, 3*, 421–423.

Drews, F. A., Yazdani, H., Godfrey, C., Cooper, J. M., & Strayer, D. L. (2009). Text messaging during simulated driving. *Human Factors, 51*, 762–770.

Eshel, N., Nelson, E.E., Blair, J., Pine, D.S., & Ernst, M. (2007). Neural substrates of choice selection in adults and adolescents: development of the ventrolateral prefrontal and anterior cingulate cortices. *Neuropsychologica, 45*(6), 1270-1279.

Foehr, U. G. (2006). *Media multitasking among American youth: Prevalence, predictors and pairings*. Washington: The Henry J. Kaiser Family Foundation.

Foerde, K., Knowlton, B. J., & Poldrack, A. (2006). Modulation of competing memory systems by distraction. *Proceedings of the National Academy of Sciences of the United States of America, 103*, 11778–11783.

Fried, C. B. (2008). In-class laptop use and its effects on student learning. *Computers & Education, 50*, 906–914.

Grossmann, I., Ellsworth, P. C., & Hong, Y. Y. (2012). Culture, attention, and emotion. *Journal of Experimental Psychology: General, 141*(1), 31.

Hedden, T., Ketay, S., Aron, A., Markus, H. R., & Gabrieli, J. D. E. (2008). Cultural influences on neural substrates of attentional control. *Psychological Science, 19*(1), 13–17.

Helder, E., & Shaughnessy, J. J. (2008). Retrieval opportunities while multitasking improve name recall. *Memory, 16*, 896–909.

Hembrooke, H., & Gay, G. (2003). The laptop and the lecture: The effects of multitasking in learning environments. *Journal of Computing in Higher Education, 15*, 46.

Hommel, B., Kessler, K., Schmitz, F., Gross, J., Akyürek, E., Shapiro, K., & Schnitzler, A. (2006). How the brain blinks: Towards a neurocognitive model of the Attentional Blink. *Psychological Research, 70*, 425-435.

Johnson, M. H. (2002). The development of visual attention: A cognitive neuroscience perspective. In Johnson, M. M., Munakata, Y., and Gilmore, R. O. (Eds.) *Brain Development and Cognition: A Reader* (134–150). Malden, MA: Blackwell Publishers.

Just, M. A., Carpenter, P. A., Keller, T. A., Emery, L., Zajac, H., & Thulborn, K. (2001). Interdependence of non-overlapping cortical systems in dual cognitive tasks. *Neuroimage, 14*, 417–426.

Kitayama, S., Duffy, S., Kawamura, T., and Larsen, J. T. (2003) Perceiving an object and its context in different cultures: A cultural look at the New Look. *Psychological Science, 14*, 201–206.

Knight, R. T. (1996). Contribution of human hippocampal region to novelty detection. *Nature, 383*, 256–259.

Lachter, J., Forster, K. I., & Ruthruff, E. (2004). Forty-five years after Broadbent: Still no identification without attention. *Psychological Review, 111*, 880–913.

Levine, L. E., Waite, B. M., & Bowman, L. L. (2007). Electronic media use, reading, and academic distractibility in college youth. *CyberPsychology & Behavior, 10*, 560–566.

Lin, L. (2009). Breadth-biased versus focused cognitive control in media multitasking behaviors. *Proceedings of the National Academy of Sciences of the United States of America, 106*, 15521–15522.

Lin, L., Robertson, T., & Lee, J. (2009). Reading performances between novices and experts in different media multitasking environments. *Computers in the Schools, 26*(3), 169-186.

Logan, G. D. (1988). Toward an instance theory of automatization. *Psychological Review, 95*, 492- 527.

MacLean, M. H., & Arnell, K. M. (2010). Personality predicts temporal attention costs in the attentional blink paradigm. *Psychonomic Bulletin & Review, 17*(4), 556–562.

Moreno, M. A., Jelenchick, L., Koff, R., Eikoff, J., Diermyer, C., & Christakis, D. A. (2012). Internet use and multitasking among older adolescents: An experience sampling approach. *Computers in Human Behavior, 28*, 1097-1102.

Newman, S. D., Keller, T. A., & Just, M. A. (2007). Volitional control of attention and brain activation in dual task performance. *Human Brain Mapping, 28*, 109-117.

Ophir, E., Nass, C., & Wagner, A.D. (2009). Cognitive control in media multitaskers. *Proceedings of the National Academy of Science, 106*(37), 15583-15587.

Posner M. I., Cohen Y., & Rafal R. D. (1982). Neural systems control of spatial orienting. *Philosophical Transactions of the Royal Society of London, Series B. 298*, 187–198.

Ray Li, C. S., Chen, S. H., Lin, W. H., & Yang, Y. Y. (2005). Attentional blink in adolescents with varying levels of impulsivity. *Journal of Psychiatric Research, 39*(2), 197–205.

Rekart, J. L. (2011). Taking on multitasking. *Phi Delta Kappan, 93*, 60–63.

Sana, F., Weston, T., & Cepeda, N. J. (2013). Laptop multitasking hinders classroom learning for both users and nearby peers. *Computers & Education, 62*, 24-31..

Schneider, W., & Chein, J.M. (2003). Controlled & automatic processing behavior, theory, and biological mechanisms. *Cognitive Science, 27*(3), 525-559.

Selikowitz, M. (2009). *ADHD*. Oxford: Oxford University Press.

Shapiro, K.L., Raymond, J.E., & Arnell, K.M. (1997). The attentional blink. *Trends in Cognitive Sciences, 1*(8), 291-296.

Shiffrin, R. M., & Schneider, W. (1977). Controlled and automatic human information processing. II. Perceptual learning, automatic attending and a general theory. *Psychological Review, 84*(2), 127–190.

Söderlund, G. B., Sikström, S., Loftesnes, J. M., & Sonuga-Barke, E. J. (2010). The effects of background white noise on memory performance in inattentive school children. *Behavioral and Brain Functions, 6*(1), 55.

Stroop, J. R. (1935). Studies of interference in verbal reactions. *Journal of Experimental Psychology, 18*, 643–662.

Sturm, W., & Willmes, K. (2001). Neuroanatomy of intrinsic and phasic alertness. *Neuroimage, 2001, 14*(1), S76-S84.

Treisman, A. (1969). Strategies and models of selective attention. *Psychological Review, 76*, 282–299.

Vogel, E. K., & Luck, S. J. (2002). Delayed working memory consolidation during the attentional blink. *Psychonomic Bulletin & Review, 9*, 739-743.

Zucker, A. A., & Light, D. (2009). Laptop programs for students. *Science, 323*(5910), 82–85.

FOUR
Working Memory

Take a moment and think about what you need to do once you finish reading this page (or chapter or perhaps the rest of the book). Done? Great. Let's examine what just happened.

Chances are good that when you began contemplating what to do next, several things occurred. You likely used your interior "voice" to "say" (i.e., your mind's "voice") or list what needed to happen. In addition, you may have pictured, in your head, using what is often referred to as your mind's "eye" (though I prefer to think of it more as a mind's "slideshow"), exactly what you need to do. Perhaps you have to travel somewhere and you could "see" it. Indeed, you may have even activated movie-like playback of a personal memory, complete with audio. And finally, when you were contemplating your list and the places you may or may not need to go, you likely didn't take note of the fact that at that time you became less aware of your surroundings.

By engaging in this little exercise, you activated the cognitive process that is the basis for this chapter: working memory. Working memory is an incredibly important process that is used whenever we learn something new, think about what to do next, or engage in reminiscence. Put simply, it is both the gateway to long-term storage of information, what we commonly think of as simply "memory," and the place where we think about our past, present, and even what we intend to do in the future.

BASICS OF WORKING MEMORY

Working memory, which is a refinement of what is also known as short-term memory (Baddeley & Hitch, 1974), is seen by many researchers as the place where new information is acted upon before it is either sent to be stored for long periods of time (long-term memory) or summarily forgotten. In the classic "three-stage" model of memory (Atkinson & Shiffrin, 1968), information from the senses is held for a brief period of time (on the order of milliseconds; i.e., sensory memory), then is either lost or passed on to short-term/working memory (which we will hereafter refer to simply as working memory or WM). Because information must first pass through WM before entering into long-term storage (the third "stage"), working memory acts as filter or gatekeeper of the information that we store throughout our lives.

One defining characteristic of working memory is its brevity. Even though you are now actively reading this book, it is likely that you cannot recall what the fifth word of this chapter was. You could probably identify what the general topic is (OK, so that's an easy one) and may even be able to broadly describe the tone or theme of the introductory paragraph, but a specific word-for-word account escapes you. Take a moment longer, but don't look back yet. The fact that you are having difficulty even though (1) you were probably engaged in the reading (how can you not be—this is great stuff!) and (2) you just read it is a byproduct of the limited life that information has in working memory. OK, now you can go and confirm for yourself that the fifth word of the chapter was in fact... "think."

This exercise illustrates the fact that if we don't actively engage in rehearsal (e.g., reciting the passage over and over again), then the lifespan of most items is no more than 30 seconds in this short-term memory store. Indeed, this also illustrates one of the distinctions between short-term and working memory, which is that short-term memory is working memory without the "work" (i.e., rehearsal). In the case of the word "think," you were certainly processing and taking each word individually into short-term memory; however, after 30 seconds or so all that you retained was the overarching theme or gist of the passage and the specific words as written were lost.

There is more to the distinction between short- and long-term memory than just the duration of the information that is stored. Indeed, long-term memory also differs from short-term/working memory in that it doesn't require conscious rehearsal mechanisms to be stored (though non-conscious brain rhythms may be necessary; Routtenberg & Rekart, 2005).

So working memory allowed for the storage of broad themes but not the specifics of each sentence. This is yet another defining characteristic of working memory: the limits of how much can be stored. Let's see for ourselves.

Get a blank piece of paper and fold it in half so that you cannot see the typed sets of letters through the paper. Now cover the letters that appear below in the pyramid so that you can only see the top set. What you will do now is read each set once, then immediately after reading the set cover it up and try to remember what each of the letters in order were (if you are able to do so, try it out loud). Once you're done with one set, then move on to the next and repeat.

SET 1:	S G R D E F
SET 2:	L C R O V W N
SET 3:	J C R B Z U M Q S
SET 4:	B N A O Z W X L E C J
SET 5:	T W P U F K D G O E Q V R

How did you do? Chances are good that you had perfect remembrance for the letters in sets one through three, partial recollection of set 4, and almost none for set 5. This prediction is based on the classic finding by George Miller from 1956 that human short-term memory can hold, without any rehearsal mechanisms or work being done, about 7 ± 2 pieces of information. Because set 4 has 11 items, it is just outside the "normal" limits but still not so large as to be impossible. Set 5, however, with 13 items, is almost double our capacity.

As we'll see shortly, the limit on the amount of information we can actively act upon or store, depending on the nature of what is being stored (e.g., is it meaningful? If a word, how long is it?), is often times no more than 4 ± 1 items (Cowan et al., 2005).

Up to this point, we have described the spatial (roughly 3–9 items) and temporal (about 30 seconds) limits of working memory but have yet to explore exactly what type of *work* is done. In 1976 Baddeley and Hitch described how information entering the spatially and temporally limited short-term store of Atkinson and Shiffrin could be held longer and earmarked for long-term storage. In their updated model, working memory has four primary components (Baddeley, 2003). Two of those components are readily experienced in our day-to-day existence.

The first to be discussed comprises our "mind's voice" and "mind's ear," known collectively as the *phonoarticulatory* loop (sometimes referred to as the phonological loop). We use our phonoarticulatory loop whenever we repeat something inside our minds to try and remember it. For example, before the advent of so-called "smart" phones, people would engage their phonoarticulatory loops to remember information like a phone number or address while they searched for paper and pen(cil) with which to record it.

The phonoarticulatory loop is used to maintain and process auditory and speech-related information. Behavioral support for its role in the processing of verbal information comes from studies that have found that the phonological aspects of information, such as how similar words sound to one another, affect the amount of information that can be stored, with more *non*-rhyming words being able to be stored than rhyming

(Baddeley, 2003). Because of their similar sounds, rhyming words interfere with one another.

Brain regions that facilitate the temporary storage of acoustic information in the phonological loop are found in the left temporal lobe and parietal regions and Broca's area in the frontal lobe, all of which are necessary for language processing and speech production (Baddeley, 2003). Thus our brain uses the same regions to say something whether it is only to ourselves using our mind's voice or if it is a declaration to the world using our actual mouths.

The second component of working memory that we can readily experience is the visuospatial sketchpad. The visuospatial sketchpad is responsible for our ability to consciously process visual or spatial (i.e., *where* something is located in the physical world) information. If I were to be shown a picture that I've never seen before and then the picture is taken away, my ability to still *see* the image in my mind, even though it has been removed, is a result of the activation of areas of my brain responsible for visual processing, including parts of the occipital cortex, as well as the right parietal and frontal lobes (Baddeley, 2003).

The processing of spatial information is facilitated by separate components of this same system. Spatial processing involves relations of objects to one another in three-dimensional space. If I mentally walk through my childhood home or think about where in my current kitchen a jar of peanut butter is stored, the recollection of previously stored information occurs within this working memory component.

Though there are individual differences in the capacity of visual working memory, which are reflected by the degree of brain activity in both the parietal and occipital lobes (Courtney, Ungerleider, Keil, & Haxby, 1997; Vogel & Machizawa, 2004), the limits to this system can be increased.

The third component of this system is the episodic buffer. The episodic buffer is localized to the left anterior hippocampus (Berlingen et al., 2008) and the dorsolateral prefrontal cortex (Baddeley, 2003). The role of the buffer is to bind together auditory, visual, and, possibly, other sensory information (i.e., touch) into one coherent scene. These scenes underlie what is known as our episodic memory and constitute what most of us think of when we talk about our "memories."

Interestingly, this binding together of various sensory elements into one unitary memory has been postulated to underlie consciousness (Baddeley, 2000). As we will see when we discuss long-term memory retrieval, because many of those same brain structures are also used when we remember something, our existing memories are modified when they are retrieved. Then we restore those memories as though they are new (Baddeley, 2003). Put differently, whenever we remember an episode from our life it is possible, and, indeed, is likely, that we modify that memory depending upon our current circumstances. This idea will be revisited (with some help from Bugs Bunny) in chapter 6.

Finally, the model of working memory we have been discussing requires a supervisor. Some region of the brain is required to direct incoming or retrieved information to the correct working memory processing site (i.e., the loop, sketchpad, or episodic buffer) to determine how long the information should be maintained and whether to discard current information in favor of new.

As you may have surmised from this description, the *central executive* of working memory is responsible for directing one's attention. Indeed, attention and working memory are often lumped together, along with reasoning, using the broad label of "executive functioning." Portions of the dorsolateral prefrontal cortex of the brain (Kane & Engle, 2002), separable from those underlying the episodic buffer, are responsible for directing attention in this manner.

The maturation of working memory is believed to be responsible for the development of other cognitive processes. For example, increases in the capacity of working memory must occur before children can begin crafting complex sentences that extend beyond just a few words. There isn't a true separation of the phonoarticulatory loop and the visuospatial sketchpad from the central executive until about six years of age. From age six well into adolescence (15 years), the capacity of the working memory components then increases linearly (Gathercole, Pickering, Ambridge, & Wearing, 2004).

Attempts have been made to examine working memory in children younger than 4. Preliminary evidence suggests that early development of the phonoarticulatory loop may underlie individual differences in language acquisition (Gathercole & Adams, 1993).

MAKING THE MOST OF A LIMITED SYSTEM

The importance of working memory for academic success cannot be overstated. As one of the foundational mental processes underlying higher order cognition, the capacity of working memory affects all higher-order cognition. From the storage of new concepts and strategies to the successful implementation and application of existing knowledge, working memory plays a role. Therefore, like attention, when working memory, with its limited capacity, is overwhelmed, cognition suffers. Therefore, it is critically important that educators are not only aware of the components of this system (see the first part of this chapter) but also are able to apply various strategies and techniques to enhance working memory.

First, we'll focus on how to make the most of the existing system that we have. That is to say, how do we manage information to make it fit within a limited system? Additionally, what techniques work to free working memory from processing unnecessary information and stimuli? In the second portion, we will examine the pedagogical ramifications of exciting developments from the past decade that suggest that working memory systems possess an underappreciated neural plasticity. Training may actually increase the capacity of both the phonoarticulatory and visuospatial stores by modifying neural connections (Klingberg, 2010). These latter findings are of particular importance given the relationship between working memory capacity and standard measures of intelligence and reasoning (Kane & Engle, 2002; Kyllonen & Christal, 1990). Indeed, recent empirical studies have even shown that training on working memory tasks increases some forms of intelligence (Jaeggi, Buschkuehl, Jonides, & Perrig, 2008).

Now let's revisit our letter pyramid exercise that we used previously. Get your piece of paper ready to cover the sets of letters because we are now going to try two more. This time, however, we will refuse to be limited by Miller's magic number for short-term memory. Rather than maxing out at 13 letters (set #5 from the first pyramid), let's push ourselves and (successfully) attempt 15! Here we go:

SET 6:   Z A T W L P U F D G O J E Q R

How did you do? Any better? If the answer is "No," don't be discouraged. We're going to try one more, but this time you may find it is a bit easier:

SET 7:   G P A P H D I N C A T M E T C

Did you remember more letters from set #7 than #6? Could you remember all of the letters from this last set? If you didn't detect any differences between 6 and 7, look at each set of letters again, but this time without the paper to cover and without worrying how many items you'll be able to recall. If you recognized that the letters in set #7 could be grouped into familiar sets of three-letter abbreviations, then you may have had an easier time recalling the fifteen items if you grouped them into the following five clusters:

(G P A) (P H D) (I N C) (A T M) (E T C)

If you didn't recognize the letters as distinct, don't worry. We'll try one more grouping, only this time you are going to remember 16 distinct bits of information. These will be numbers and as you are reading them try to find a pattern or grouping principle that you could use. Ready? Here we go:

SET 8:   1 7 7 6 1 8 1 2 1 4 9 2 1 9 8 4

How many were you able to remember now? If you recognized that the 16 numbers could be grouped as four dates [(1776)(1812)(1492)(1984)], then you likely had no problems remembering the 4 items. This process is called "chunking" and represents a very simple and successful way to work around the capacity limits of working memory. Note that it doesn't matter if the digits are actually dates or not. All that matters is your ability to remember the 16 pieces of information using one work of British fiction and three salient dates from American history (and in our examination of both long-term memory encoding and retrieval, we will discuss clues for why it is that when most of you hear the date "1492" you can't help but finish with the sing-song recitation that "Columbus sailed the ocean blue").

Why is chunking useful? It is of use because the longer you can hold items in working memory or the more items you can store, the greater the possibility for long-term storage. Think about a phone number. Luckily we know that a phone number is parsed into three components: the area code, the first three digits (i.e., the prefix), and after the dash, the last four digits. This parsing is helpful, particularly as we can often disregard the area code, and if we know of somebody else with a similar prefix, we can just think of that person (one unit of information rather than three individual numbers) along with the last four.

For the teacher, chunking could be used when presenting concepts or pieces of information that have to be known. A caveat about the chunks, however, is that they cannot be so large that they cease to function as independent units. For example, word list #1 (in the following example) is likely to be remembered better than #2, even though both lists contain the exact same number of words.

LIST #1:   CAT NOD HIM DIE BUD
LIST #2:   CATALOGUE NODULAR
              HIMSELF DIETARY BUDGETED

The difference in memorizability between lists #1 and #2 is a result of what is known as the word-length effect, and it is directly related to the number of syllables contained within each word (Baddeley, Thomson, & Buchanan, 1975). The syllables matter because this type of chunking is utilizing the phonoarticulatory loop and, thus, the amount of time required to say each word using one's mind's voice will limit the number of words that can be remembered. Because of the limits of the phonoarticulatory loop, it has also been shown that list #1 will be remembered better than list #3 (in the following example):

LIST #3:   CAT NOT DOT HAT BAT

It is more difficult to store list #3 because some of the words rhyme with one another (cat, hat, and bat; not and dot). The rhyming words interfere and even blend with one another within our minds, thus creating difficulties when we try to remember any specific individual word. Indeed, the fact that rhymes are not effective mnemonic strategies runs counter to the beliefs of many individuals (Park, Smith, & Cavanaugh, 1990) but is consistent with evidence from research that showed that rhymes were not particularly effective mnemonic techniques (e.g., Craik & Tulving, 1975).

Regardless of the number of syllables or whether the chunked information rhymes or not, chunking only works if there is meaning. Information only has meaning if there is a match between the (chunked) stimuli and a representation in long-term memory. For example, you are more likely to be able to chunk the numbers 3 1 4 than 1 6 1 as the mathematical constant π (3.1415 . . .) is more universally learned than the so-called golden ratio (1.6180 . . .). Thus if you don't recognize the numbers 1 4 9 2 from set #8 as a date (or if you are from a country where that particular date in time isn't of any particular significance), then the chunks aren't of any use.

The use of meaningful chunks frees attentional resources so that more capacity will be available for actual storage. In the classroom, this is important to remember so that cognitive resources aren't unnecessarily dedicated to items that aren't directly related to the concepts or strategies to be learned. Let's look at a hypothetical word problem that closely resembles those often seen in early math textbooks:

> A bag contains 15 marbles. 4 of the marbles are green, 6 of the marbles are blue, and 5 of the marbles are red. If Timmy reaches into the bag, what color marble is he most likely to grab?

Though there is nothing mathematically wrong with this example, in the 21st century such situations are rarely, if ever, encountered. Thus though children of yesteryear were likely to have bags of marbles, in today's world this anachronistic story won't be readily familiar to all children. The result? That working memory capacity will be devoted to understanding what a bag of marbles looks like—actually imagining it and so forth—which will deplete working memory stores needed to actually apply concepts of relative quantity as well as how those concepts apply to probability.

What is needed in this circumstance is a word problem or example that actually draws upon the experiences of all children. As with most phenomena, this is not a "cut-and-dry" recommendation as novelty, meaning strikingly different or discordant stimuli, are remembered readily. However, one must not confuse novelty with unfamiliarity, as the latter will stifle memory storage as readily as the former will enhance it. Ideally, word problems such as the one given previously will both refrain from taxing working memory and, if at all possible, introduce sufficient novelty to enhance remembrance.

In 1998 Mayer and Moreno demonstrated that college students who were presented scientific images with the words narrated rather than written on the screen did better on tests of recall and transfer than those who both viewed the images and read textual information about the images (i.e., captions). Among others, Goolkasian and Foos (2002), using a different paradigm, found similar results for what is known as the "modality effect"; namely, that words that are presented auditorily are remembered better than those that are written.

These findings may be because when we hear the words we have to activate our own mind's ear and thus introduce the possibility of active rehearsal through repetition within the phonoarticulatory loop. Alternatively, it could be a byproduct of the automaticity of reading. Regardless, it should be noted that optimal encoding of information in working memory will likely be obtained through narration rather than the reading of textual information.

Though it has been discussed previously in this book, it is important to note that studies such as those just discussed don't sort research participants based on some kind of perceptual learning style (e.g., "visual" or "auditory" learner), but rather all participants were randomly exposed to one modality or another (i.e., either to the visual images + visual words or visual images + auditory words). Despite this inattention to "individual differences," students still do better when the two sensory modalities (i.e., auditory and visual) were used together. Such findings reiterate the need to focus on general, empirically research-based, or, in this case, research-validated, claims regarding learning (e.g., Pashler, McDaniel, Rohrer, & Bjork, 2008) rather than those that rely on conjecture and speculation—no matter how popular they may be.

When presenting information, it may be useful to alternate verbal and visual information to provide enough time for the memory in either repository to be stored before moving on to new stimuli. Because the phonoarticulatory loop and the visuospatial sketchpad operate independently of one another and largely derive from separable brain regions, they can be concurrently used without one impeding the abilities of the other (Baddeley, 2003).

The notion of one working memory system interfering with another has important ramifications for instruction, particularly mathematics. As was discussed, the working memory system develops throughout early childhood and into adolescence (Gathercole, Pickering, Ambridge, & Wearing, 2004). Correspondingly, the way in which children of different age groups process simple arithmetic changes over the early development of the system.

McKenzie, Bull, and Gray (2003) found that though younger children (ages six to seven) primarily relied on the visuospatial sketchpad to solve math problems, older children (ages 8 and up) utilize the phonoarticulatory system. When teaching math from around second grade forward, it is important to remember that spoken language will interfere with the processing of math. Put differently, speech, distracting sounds, and so forth will interfere with mental calculations in a way that visual distractors will not. Thus, though group work is useful in many contexts, low working-memory students may benefit from fewer auditory distractions that will leave more mental processing capacity to actually perform the math in their heads.

Competition for individual working memory stores is an important consideration. Switching between different categories of information, even information that uses the same working memory store, also works to free working memory capacity. In a classic paper from 1941, Young and Supa showed that short lists that had digits and words:

$$4\ 7\ 9\ 2\ \text{whale}$$

were better remembered than lists that contained information of all the same type:

$$4\ 7\ 9\ 2\ 1$$

These findings have subsequently been replicated numerous times (e.g., Bunting, 2006), and the difference in recall ability is a result of a phenomenon known as *proactive interference*.

Proactive interference occurs when previously stored information interferes with newer information (e.g., Lustig, Hasher, & May, 2001). The previously stored information, which is believed to reside in long-term memory, can either become confused with the new or it can just impede recall altogether. This is demonstrated in working memory tasks when one attempts to remember a number of lists of words that are semantically similar (e.g., Bunting, 2006). For example, let's say we were learning three lists of animals, grouped by ecosystem/where they are commonly found.

List 1:	COW HORSE SHEEP GOAT PIG DOG
List 2:	CAMEL LIZARD SNAKE TORTOISE RAT FOX
List 3:	WHALE CORAL SHARK DOLPHIN FISH SPONGE

If presented in the same session, the words on the first list will be remembered best, the words on the second will be remembered less well, and those on the third list will be the most impaired. However, if the words in one of the lists were to be changed categorically (see revised list 2) so that the proactive interference would be disrupted and memory wouldn't be impaired.

Revised List 2: SHIRT HAT PURSE SHOE PANTS WATCH

Instructional examples should be sufficiently varied so that examples or problems shown first don't interfere with those worked or shown later. Because children older than eight largely rely on the phonoarticulatory loop for mathematical calculations (McKenzie, Bull, & Gray, 2003), this recommendation even applies to math problems. It may be useful to vary problems so that they tap into different working memory stores so as to reduce proactive interference.

The ability to discard unneeded information from working memory is critical for success in applying existing knowledge (i.e., only remembering pertinent facts and strategies) and for the long-term storage of new information (i.e., only focusing on what is important). Poor working memory skills in some individuals may be a byproduct of an inability to separate informational wheat from chaff. These individuals use up memory capacity with useless distractions or trivial aspects of information (Vogel, McCollough, & Machizawa, 2005).

This aspect of working memory, the selection of information to be acted upon, falls under the jurisdiction of the central executive. If one were to be able to reduce or inhibit competing bits of information, it could enhance this functionality in lower-functioning individuals. Indeed, the ability to inhibit unneeded information has been linked to academic success in language arts, mathematics, and scientific reasoning (St-Clair Thompson & Gathercole, 2006).

EMOTION AND WORKING MEMORY

When we have an emotional reaction to news, a situation, or a person, working memory resources and attention are shifted away from the cognitive tasks we may be engaged in to allow us to understand and experience our emotions. Thus when we are worried or concerned about how well we will do academically, we take resources away that we need to succeed. This emotional interference has been seen with, among other things, math anxiety (Ashkraft & Krause, 2007).

The interfering effect of a condition like math anxiety upon working memory is likely due to an inability to prevent distracting stimuli from depleting working memory resources (Hopko et al., 1998). In order to combat math, or other education-related anxiety, it is incumbent upon the teacher to create an atmosphere of acceptance. Though this seems like a "no-brainer," what is meant here is beyond the acceptance of the student and extends into the curriculum itself. The mistakes of calculating need to be seen as not merely "OK" but as routine and part of life.

Indeed, by modeling famous mathematicians who were wrong or by communicating to the students that only through trial and error does learning occur, a climate where it is OK to make an attempt will be created.

However, it isn't just students with anxiety who are affected by the impact of emotion on cognition. Beilock and Carr (2005) showed that students with good working memory capacities, but not those with poor working memory spans, were impaired under conditions of overt pressure to succeed. These results were counterintuitive to the assumption that pressure would interfere most with those who are already disadvantaged. Beilock and Carr hypothesized that students with strong working memory capacities probably are used to getting the most from their cognitive resources. However, because feelings of anxiety are known to strain working memory capacity, these students had fewer resources available to them, making them more susceptible to memory impairments.

We as teachers need to be aware of the fact that we cannot just assume that higher-functioning students are able to "cope" with pressure. We need to avoid, when possible, creating undue burdens upon high achievers by puffing up expectations for their success—even with seemingly supportive statements such as "Of course, you'll ace this test" or "A student like you won't have any problems."

INCREASING WORKING MEMORY CAPACITY

It should now be apparent that working memory deficits have far-reaching implications for academic success. The limited capacity of the system, even in high-functioning individuals, places restrictions on the quantity and quality of information that can be retained and the pace with which it can be learned. As outlined in the preceding sections, knowledge of how working memory actually operates can be used to optimize curriculum and instruction to avoid proactive interference and facilitate chunking of information. While useful, what would be of maximum benefit would be the ability to also increase the storage potential of this system. The ability to expand the capacity of students with working memory impairments would go a long way in facilitating their success in school settings.

Empirical reports have recently started to emerge that convincingly demonstrate that working memory *can* be enhanced using relatively short-term, intensive training programs. These programs last for less than an hour a day (usually between 30 and 45 minutes per session). The training programs that have been used to date have utilized proprietary software that provides exercises designed to alternately train verbal working memory (i.e., the phonoarticulatory loop), visuospatial working memory, and the allocation of attentional resources (i.e., the central executive). After about five weeks of training, children with general working memory deficits (in the 15th percentile), with (Klingberg et al., 2005) or without (Holmes, Gathercole, & Dunning, 2009) a diagnosis of attention-deficit/hyperactivity disorder (ADHD), saw sizable gains. Amazingly, the training benefits, increases in both visuospatial and verbal working memory, were still evident six months after the training had ceased.

How would working memory training leads to lasting cognitive benefits? Jaeggi, Buschkuehl, Jonides, and Perrig (2008) found that working memory training actually leads to increases in what is known as fluid intelligence, which doesn't relate to the storage of facts but rather the application of knowledge (i.e., reasoning). Such changes may be the result of working memory training-induced modifications in brain structures that underlie the allocation of resources to different working memory systems.

Klingberg, Forssberg, and Westerberg (2002) demonstrated that working memory training designed to expand the visuospatial sketchpad resulted in increases in activity in both the frontal and parietal lobes, both of which are brain regions known to be responsible for this working memory process (Baddeley, 2003). However, other researchers have also found that some training of this sort results in decreases in brain activity (c.f. Klingberg, 2010). Though these may seem like contradictory findings, the decreases, in fact, are believed to underlie the automaticity of some practices, for example rehearsal mechanisms, that may not have been used as much before the training. The increases, on the other hand, likely reflect the expanded ability to handle new types of information with flexibility, which would allow the central executive to increase the effectiveness of other working memory processes.

Given such results, why don't all schools implement broad-based working memory–enhancing software? For starters, the costs of many commercially available programs are prohibitive. In addition, proper implementation of the software requires personnel trained in the application and proper interpretation of the data. In an extensive online study, Owen and colleagues (2010) demonstrated that there were few, if any, benefits seen from the online (free) usage of a web-based cognitive training program. These seemingly conflicting (to others reviewed previously) results have been logically interpreted as being consequences of the (1) broad nature of the exercises in the web-based program (i.e., it wasn't tailored specifically to enhance working memory but rather a wide range of cognitive abilities), (2) the lack of oversight for individuals involved in the "training" who could log on whenever and wherever they felt like it, and (3) the average amount of time spent in "training" (approximately 10 minutes or so) per session (Klingberg, 2010; Owen et al., 2010).

In summary, though there are some intriguing evidence-validated "hints" of the ability to expand working memory through computer-based training programs, the price of such programs (which are not covered by insurance) is such that they will remain out of touch for most educators and districts. Given the restricted use and/or availability of such programs, it is paramount that educators follow the recommendations listed in this chapter. These recommendations are based on sound research on working memory, which demonstrates how to expand what can be contained within the existing limits of the working memory stores of students.

POINTS TO REMEMBER:

- Working memory, which relies on attention, is the gatekeeper for information that will be remembered long term.
- Adult working memory can only store, depending upon the type of information, from three to nine items simultaneously. Without consciously thinking about these items (i.e., the "work" in "working" memory), they will be forgotten in about 30 seconds.
- Working memory has four components: the phonoarticulatory loop, the visuospatial sketchpad, the episodic buffer, and the central executive, all of which rely on different brain structures.
- The amount of information that can be contained within working memory can be increased by making meaningful "chunks" that group together individual items into larger, cohesive units.
- Textual information is remembered better when it is heard rather than when it is read.
- Avoid using large groups of words or numbers that are semantically similar, that rhyme, or that have too many syllables as these will reduce the working memory capacity of the phonoarticulatory loop.
- Present information so that it doesn't overload working memory. This can be accomplished by tapping into both the visuospatial sketchpad and the phonoarticulatory loop.
- Emotion drains resources and capacity from working memory.
- The limits of working memory may be able to be increased through daily, intensive computerized training using special exercises designed to target the visuospatial sketchpad, phonoarticulatory loop, and central executive.

REFERENCES

Ashcraft, M.H., & Krause, J.A. (2007). Working memory, math performance, and math anxiety. *Psychonomic Bulletin & Review*, 14(2), 243-248.

Atkinson, R. C., & Shiffrin, R. M. (1968). Human memory: A proposed system and its control processes. In K. W. Spence & J. T. Spence (Eds.), *The psychology of learning and motivation: Advances in research and theory* (Vol. 2; pp. 90–197). New York: Academic Press.

Baddeley, A. D. (2000). The episodic buffer: A new component of working memory? *Trends in Cognitive Sciences, 4*(11), 417–423.

Baddeley, A. D. (2003). Working memory: Looking back and looking forward. *Nature Reviews Neuroscience, 4*, 829–839.

Baddeley, A. D., & Hitch, G. (1974). Working memory. In G. H. Bower (Ed.), *The psychology of learning and motivation: Advances in research and theory* (Vol. 8; pp. 47–89). New York: Academic Press.

Baddeley, A. D., Thomson, N., & Buchanan, M. (1975). Word length and the structure of short-term memory. *Journal of Verbal Learning and Verbal Behavior, 14*, 575–589.

Beilock, S. L., & Carr, T. H. (2005). When high-powered people fail: Working memory and "choking under pressure" in math. *Psychological Science, 16*, 101–105.

Berlingeri, M., Bottini, G., Basilico, S., Silani, G., Zanardi, G., Sberna, M., Colombo, N., Sterzi, R., Scialfa, G., & Paulesu, E. (2008). Anatomy of the episodic buffer: a voxel-based morphometry study in patients with dementia. *Behavioural Neurology, 19*, 29-34.

Bunting, M. (2006). Proactive interference and item similarity in working memory. *Journal of Experimental Psychology: Learning, Memory, & Cognition, 32*, 183–196.

Courtney, S. M., Ungerleider, L. G., Keil, K., & Haxby, J. V. (1997). Transient and sustained activity in a distributed neural system for human working memory. *Nature, 386*, 608–611.

Cowan, N., Elliott, E. M., Scott Saults, J., Morey, C. C., Mattox, S., Hismjatullina, A., & Conway, A. R. (2005). On the capacity of attention: Its estimation and its role in working memory and cognitive aptitudes. *Cognitive Psychology, 51*(1), 42–100.

Craik, F. I. M., & Tulving, E. (1975). Depth of processing and the retention of words in episodic memory. *Journal of Experimental Psychology: General, 104*, 268-294.

Daneman, M., & Carpenter, A. (1980). Individual differences in working memory and reading. *Journal of Verbal Learning and Verbal Behavior, 19*, 450–466.

Gathercole, S. E. & Adams, A. (1993). Phonological working memory in very young children. *Developmental Psychology, 29*(4), 770–778.

Gathercole, S. E., Pickering, S. J., Ambridge, B., & Wearing, H. (2004). The structure of working memory from 4 to 15 years of age. *Developmental Psychology, 40*, 177–190.

Goolkasian, P., & Foos, P. W. (2002). Presentation format and its effect on working memory. *Memory & Cognition, 30*, 1096–1105.

Hitch, G.J., & Baddeley, A.D. (1976). Verbal reasoning and working memory. *The Quarterly Journal of Experimental Psychology, 28*(4), 603-621.

Holmes, J., Gathercole, S. E., & Dunning, D. L. (2009). Adaptive training leads to sustained enhancement of poor working memory in children. *Developmental Psychology, 12*, F9–F15.

Hopko, D. R., Ashcraft, M. H., Gute, J., Ruggiero, K. J., & Lewis, C. (1998). Mathematics anxiety and working memory: Support for the existence of a deficient inhibition mechanism. *Journal of Anxiety Disorders, 12*(4), 343–355.

Jaeggi, S. M., Buschkuehl, M., Jonides, J., & Perrig, W. J. (2008). Improving fluid intelligence with training on working memory. *Proceedings of the National Academy of Sciences of the United States of America, 105*(19), 6829–6833.

Kane, M. J., & Engle, R. W. (2002). The role of prefrontal cortex in working-memory capacity, executive attention, and general fluid intelligence: An individual-differences perspective. *Psychonomic Bulletin & Review, 9*, 637–671.

Klingberg, T., Forssberg, H., & Westerberg, H. (2002). Increased brain activity in frontal and parietal cortex underlies the development of visuospatial working memory capacity during childhood. *Journal of Cognitive Neuroscience, 14*(1), 1–10.

Klingberg, T., Fernell, E., Olesen, P. J., Johnson, M., Gustafsson, P., Dahlstrom, K., Gillberg, C. G., Forssberg, H., & Westerberg, H. (2005). Computerised training of working memory in children with ADHD: A randomised controlled trial. *Journal of the American Academy of Child and Adolescent Psychiatry*, 44, 177–186.

Klingberg, T. (2010). Training and plasticity of working memory. *Trends in Cognitive Sciences*, 14, 317–324.

Kyllonen, P. C., & Christal, R. E. (1990). Reasoning ability is (little more than) working memory capacity. *Intelligence*, 14, 389–433.

Loosli, S. V., Buschkuehl, M., Perrig, W. J., & Jaeggi, S. M. (2012). Working memory training improves reading processes in typically developing children. *Child Neuropsychology: A Journal on Normal and Abnormal Development in Childhood and Adolescence*, 18(1), 62–78.

Lustig, C., Hasher, L., & May, C.P. (2001). Working memory span and the role of proactive interference. *Journal of Experimental Psychology: General*, 130(2), 199-207.

Mayer, R. E. & Moreno, R. (1998). A split-attention effect in multimedia learning: Evidence for dual-processing systems in working memory. *Journal of Educational Psychology*, 90, 312–320.

McKenzie, B., Bull, R., & Gray, C. (2003). The effects of phonological and visual-spatial interference on children's arithmetical performance. *Educational and Child Psychology*, 20(3), 93–108.

Miller, G. A. (1956). The magical number seven, plus or minus two: Some limits on our capacity for processing information. *Psychological Review*, 63, 81–97.

Olesen, P. J., Westerberg, H., & Klingberg, T. (2004). Increased prefrontal and parietal activity after training of working memory. *Nature Neuroscience*, 7, 75–79.

Owen, A.M., Hampshire, A., Grahn, J.A., Stenton, R., Dajani, S., Burns, A.S., Howard, R.J., & Ballard, C.G. (2010). Putting brain training to the test. *Nature*, 465(7299), 775-778.

Park, D. C., Smith, A. D., & Cavanaugh, J. C. (1990). Metamemories of memory researchers. *Memory & Cognition*, 18(3), 321–327.

Pashler, H., McDaniel, M., Rohrer, D., & Bjork, R. (2008). Learning styles: Concepts and evidence. *Psychological Science in the Public Interest*, 9, 105–119.

Routtenberg, A., & Rekart, J. L. (2005). Post-translational protein modification as the substrate for long-lasting memory. *Trends in Neurosciences*, 28(1), 12–19.

Smith, E. E., Jonides, J., and Koeppe, R. A. (1996). Dissociating verbal and spatial working memory using PET. *Cerebral Cortex*, 6, 11-20.

St Clair-Thompson, H.L., & Gathercole, S.E. (2006). Executive functions and achievements in school: Shifting, updating, inhibition, and working memory. *The Quarterly Journal of Experimental Psychology*, 59(4), 745-759.

Vogel, E. K., & Luck, S. J. (2002). Delayed working memory consolidation during the attentional blink. *Psychonomic Bulletin & Review*, 9(4), 739–743.

Vogel, E. K., & Machizawa, M. G. (2004). Neural activity predicts individual differences in visual working memory capacity. *Nature*, 428(6984), 748–751.

Vogel, E. K., McCollough, A. W., & Machizawa, M. G. (2005). Neural measures reveal individual differences in controlling access to working memory. *Nature*, 438(7067), 500–503.

Young, C. W., & Supa, M. (1941). Mnemonic inhibition as a factor in the limitation of the memory span. *American Journal of Psychology*, 54, 546–552.

FIVE

Long-term Memory Encoding

Whereas the duration of working memory is on the order of seconds or, at most, minutes, we have the ability to recall information in the long term, meaning hours, days, years, and even decades after something has occurred or a concept was learned. Most often when we talk about long-term memory, we speak of dates, events, facts, and scenes from our lives. However, what we often fail to realize is that the skills that we carry with us, from walking to writing to driving a car, are also a byproduct of memory. Although we will be primarily, if not exclusively, concerned with the former form of memory (given its central role in academic success), we must recognize that the generic term *memory* is actually a broad category of similar, though dissociable, processes that all result in the long-term storage of information for later use.

TYPES OF LONG-TERM MEMORY

So what are the different forms of long-term memory? Long-term memory can be divided into two broad categories: non-declarative and declarative (Squire & Zola, 1996).[1] Non-declarative memories are those for which learning takes place by *doing* rather than by *knowing*. Memory is subsequently demonstrated by doing (rather than saying, or "declaring") as well. As anyone who has ever tried to learn how to swing a golf club or drive a car with a stick shift knows, the only true way to learn and master the skill is through the trial and error of doing. The skills that are learned on the golf course or the road are stored as procedural memories. Indeed, even higher-order skills like reading are procedural memories (which is one, of many, reasons why learning to read is such a challenging endeavor).

Other types of non-declarative memories include classical conditioning and priming. Classical, or Pavlovian, conditioning refers to the linking together of natural responses (i.e., unconditioned responses) with stimuli that do not normally elicit the response (i.e., the conditioned stimulus). You are most likely familiar with the classic studies conducted by Ivan Pavlov in which he demonstrated that by repeatedly pairing the sound of a bell ringing with the delivery of a meal (in this case it was "meat paste" . . . don't try to imagine it), dogs would begin to salivate when just the bell alone was rung—regardless if they could smell the expected meal or not.

A hallmark of classical conditioning is that the conditioned response occurs without deliberate intention on the part of the learner. It is conscious intent that differentiates classical conditioning from another form of long-term, associative, non-declarative memory: operant conditioning. Operant, or Skinnerian, conditioning involves the pairing of a stimulus with a known response that is successful in evoking the behavior. Put differently, operant conditioning occurs when a stimulus motivates us to perform and/or repeat a given behavior.

From Skinner's pigeons who would press a bar to receive a food reward, to gamblers who push the glowing buttons on electronic slot machines in hopes of a huge pay-out, to children in a daycare saying "please" to receive a sticker, operant conditioning occurs and is utilized all around us. This form of learning is non-declarative because the relationship between the antecedent stimulus and consequential response must be developed over time; thus, one must experience the pairings together.

Finally, priming is the other main form of long-term, non-declarative memory that has been extensively studied. Priming occurs when information that has been previously learned in some way modifies a future behavior. The key is that memory is influenced even though the information wasn't learned for that purpose.

For example, let's say you read the low-frequency (meaning doesn't occur often in conversation or print) word CONQUISTADOR. Then later in the chapter, you were asked to fill in the missing letters to form a word as shown in the following example:

$$C\_\_Q\_\_\_T\_\_O\_$$

If you hadn't seen the word CONQUISTADOR previously, the likelihood of solving this puzzle would likely be quite low. Chances are good that most of you (unless you're a social studies teacher) haven't thought of or seen this word in years, if not decades, which would make solving the problem very difficult. However, because you *did* see it, more of you would be able to correctly complete the word, due to priming, than would individuals who were not exposed to the word previously.

Though priming is, in a way, more directly related to memory retrieval, it is mentioned here due to its inclusion as a non-declarative memory subtype. Because declarative memory is the focus of the remainder of this chapter and many subsequent chapters within this book, please note that for the sake of brevity, from this point forward the term "long-term memory" will be used to mean "long-term declarative memory." When non-declarative memory does need to be mentioned, it will be referred to as "long-term non-declarative memory."

Unlike non-declarative memories, memories of the declarative type actually require some form of re-telling, or "declaring," to demonstrate learning. There are only two subtypes of long-term declarative memory: semantic and episodic. Semantic memory refers to all of the knowledge that we have obtained about the world, regardless if we have experienced it or not. Episodic memory, on the other hand, is comprised of all of the stored scenes that we have experienced in our lives.

Although I personally *experienced* being born, I do not (nor does anyone else) have any mental recollection of the actual act of being delivered into the world. Thus, though I know that my birthday is March 24th (cards are always appreciated), it is a semantic memory because I don't have any valid mental imagery to go along with it (nor do I want any).

Though episodic and semantic memory can be distinct, it is notable that all of our semantic knowledge of the world was gained through various episodes of our lives. What this means is that for every semantic memory that we have stored, at some point in time we also had a corresponding episodic memory that was related to the experience of *learning* the semantic information. Unfortunately, as we will see, very few episodic memories are actually retained throughout our lives. Indeed, much of the storage capacity of our minds, as amazing as it is, is taken up with semantic and not episodic information.

The average American school year consists of 180 school days. If the average (non-kindergarten) school day is roughly seven hours, with five and a half hours dedicated solely to instructional time, then after twelve years of formal schooling, the average American adult has experienced (allowing for 10 sick days a year) a minimum of 11,220 hours of schooling. This educational time resulted in a rich tapestry of knowledge that allows one to answer questions that range from who the second president of the United States was to how to apply the quadratic formula to the name of the process responsible for turning light into usable energy by plants.

But don't take my word for it, take a moment and try to think of the myriad and sundry facts that you have personally accumulated over your own elementary and secondary school years. With over ten thousand hours under your belt, there is likely to be a great deal that you know. Now try to remember when, where, and how you learned each of those facts. Can you remember the exact moment a teacher showed you that 4/6 could be reduced to 2/3?

Chances are good that you have few, if any, actual episodic memories that correspond to those moments when you obtained the information that you now carry with you. The memory for the specific moment when you learned that 4/6 was the same as 2/3 is likely lost. You can probably picture the teacher from whom you learned this, and his/her classroom, but the odds that you can recall the actual moment, complete with audio and visual information, are infinitesimally low.

Therefore, most of formal (and informal, for that matter) education results in modifications and additions to semantic memory. The previous demonstration is critical because too often educators get "turned off" when memory is spoken of as a collection of facts and skills. After all, doesn't the "modern" teacher eschew rote memorization of facts in favor of establishing deep learning? The answer to this question is both "yes" and "no." Given the nature of long-term memory, as illustrated earlier, much of education actually will result in the storage of facts and skills that are divorced from the context in which they were taught. However, it is how those facts are stored within semantic memory that makes the difference between learning for "regurgitation" (ewwww) and learning for transfer (hooray).

STAGES OF LONG-TERM MEMORY

Long-term memory, be it declarative or non-declarative, is comprised of three stages. The first stage, *encoding*, is what is most commonly referred to as learning. It is during this step that incoming information is transferred from working memory stores (remember these from the last chapter: the phonoarticulatory loop, visuospatial sketchpad, and episodic buffer) to longer-term storage sites. This transfer takes place both figuratively and literally, as brain regions not associated with working memory are recruited for the encoding of declarative information into long-term memory (i.e., medial temporal lobe regions, including the hippocampus).

The next stage, *storage*, occurs when the information is warehoused within various regions of the brain. This stage most closely resembles what people think of when they talk of memory. It should be noted that this form of storage is different from the temporary cache that is working memory because in long-term memory information is stored even though it is not the subject of conscious thought or awareness.

As we will discuss soon, the actual storage of information is a byproduct of the changes in the number, strength, and location of connections within the brain that accompany learning (encoding). Furthermore, though the "storage" within the brain is likely not a passive endeavor, but requires active maintenance of brain connections (see Rekart & Routtenberg, 2008), for our purposes we will differentiate between the act of *storing* the information initially, which is actually encoding, and the process of maintaining the stored information within the brain, which is storage.

Finally, memory is only of use so long as it can be remembered. *Retrieval*, the third stage, encompasses our ability to actually use the information that we have stored. This stage will be the focus of our next chapter, in which we will discuss the factors involved, the similarities to encoding, and the ways that educators can use that information to facilitate retrieval.

BRAIN STRUCTURES RESPONSIBLE FOR ENCODING

There are a number of brain regions responsible for the encoding of declarative information into long-term memory. Not surprisingly, some areas that are necessary for working memory continue to be used for the long-term encoding of information. One, the prefrontal cortex, plays a critical role in long-term memory formation (Blumenfeld & Ranganath, 2007). Interestingly, the two hemispheres of the brain may process information differently. The left hemisphere is preferentially involved in the storage of verbal information and the right hemisphere is involved in the storage of scenes, pictures, and nonverbal information (Buckner, Kelley, & Petersen, 1999).

This information should not, however, be taken as evidence for the notion that some students are "left-brained" and others "right-brained" if they learn better using text or images, respectively. Indeed, such labels really should be avoided because there is no real basis in the neuroscientific literature to support them (Goswami, 2006). First, though the right hemisphere does become preferentially activated for some scenes and images, it is important to note that there is bilateral (i.e., both hemispheres) activation when the scene or image has a name that can be readily called to mind (Kelley et al., 1998). Both hemispheres of the brain work in concert when you see a picture of known and familiar people, places, and things.

Second, though verbal information is preferentially encoded by the left frontal cortex, it is actually retrieved by corresponding regions located in the *right* frontal cortex (Habib, Nyberg, & Tulving, 2003). Therefore, both hemispheres must be co-operational so that information that is learned (encoding) may be used (retrieval). Finally, let us not forget that anatomically there are enormous bundles of axons that connect the left and right hemispheres, such as the corpus callosum, which enables the brain to operate as a whole despite any hemispheric division of labor.

Lying within the interior portion of the brain (i.e., toward the middle), there is one structure within the medial temporal lobe that has been demonstrated as being critically important for the encoding of long-term declarative information: the hippocampus. Our current understanding of the incredible importance of the hippocampus to the acquisition of information to be stored indefinitely can be traced back to the seminal description of the patient H. M. by Scoville and Milner in 1957.

In 1953 H. M. (at the age of 27) underwent drastic, experimental neurosurgery at the Montreal Neurological Institute to ameliorate a severe case of temporal lobe epilepsy. The operation involved removing his hippocampus from both sides of the brain. The epilepsy was so debilitating to H. M. in his daily life that the radical procedure which was performed was seen as the only way to provide any relief. Though the procedure was successful in reducing the severity and frequency of seizures, there was a dramatic and lasting side effect: the surgery left H. M. completely unable to formulate any new long-term memories (Scoville & Milner, 1957).

The inability to form new long-term memories is referred to as anterograde amnesia. This form of amnesia differs from the amnesia that occurs when one is unable to recall events from their past (*retrograde* amnesia), which is a form of amnesia that seems to occur with a high regularity on daytime soap operas.[2] Though his short-term memory was left intact (probably because the frontal lobes were not affected by the surgery), H. M. was completely unable to encode any new episodic or semantic memories. Despite the surgery, he was able to learn any number of new forms of non-declarative skills, such as mirror tracing, because those forms of learning do not rely on the hippocampus for long-term storage. However, because he was unable to form new episodic memories, he was completely unaware of the level of expertise that he had achieved (Corkin, 2002).

Thus, beginning with the study of patient H. M. and others like him, researchers began to appreciate the importance of the hippocampus for memory storage. For example, Wilder Penfield, the neurosurgeon upon whose work Scoville's procedure on H. M. was based, was able to evoke vivid memories from epileptic patients by electrically stimulating their temporal lobes while they were undergoing neurosurgery (which takes place while the patient is awake; Penfield, 1958). Thanks to non-invasive brain imaging techniques, like fMRI and PET, we now know that even in intact individuals (i.e., those who have not undergone neurosurgery) the hippocampus and other medial temporal lobe structures are necessary for long-term memory.

The hippocampus processes different forms of information (i.e., verbal and nonverbal) separately and then likely integrates those together to form a cohesive memory (Small, Nava, Perrera, DeLaPaz, Mayeux, & Stern, 2001). The information that is received by the hippocampus comes from many different cortical regions that travel through the parahippocampal gyrus, a region that is also important for the encoding of long-term memory (Brewer, Zhao, Desmond, Glover, & Gabrieli, 1998). There is some evidence to suggest that it is the synchronized activation of many medial temporal structures with the hippocampus that results in whether a memory will be successfully encoded or not (Fell, Klaver, Lehnertz, Grunwald, Schaller, Elger, & Fernandez, 2001; Fell, Ludowig, Rosburg, Axmacher, & Elger, 2008).

BRAIN PLASTICITY AND MEMORY ENCODING

It has been theorized since the time of the great neuroanatomist and Nobel laureate, Santiago Ramón y Cajal (1911), that memory must be the byproduct of changes that take place to and within the connections of the brain. This same idea was later put forth by Donald Hebb (1949) in his seminal work "The Organization of Behavior," in which he outlined the type of activity that would be necessary to produce long-lasting changes to the brain. His straightforward idea was that "repeated and persistent" use of neurons would result in changes to them that would lead to the permanent and portable storage of memory. This idea is so important to our modern understanding of how the brain stores information that Hebb's text has been mentioned as being as influential to modern science as Darwin's "On the Origin of Species" (Adams, 1998).

The types of changes that Hebb envisioned, and that we now know to be true, included those that involve physiological changes, meaning changes in the underlying electrical properties of axons and dendrites, as well as physical changes to the axons and dendrites themselves. Regardless of the type of changes, what remains at the heart of "Hebb's postulate" is that there is repeated and persistent activity.

Let's put this all together. We know that the hippocampus (as well as portions of the frontal cortex) are necessary for long-term memory encoding. And, per Hebb's postulate, brain cells in regions responsible for memory encoding need to be stimulated repeatedly. So what constitutes repeated stimulation? The easiest answer to this question is actively engaging in learning and relearning whatever is to be remembered. If you have ever had to memorize lines of a Shakespearean play or the identities and locations of elements on the periodic table, then you probably engaged in repeated and persistent activation.

The way you most likely learned the next line after, "Whether 'tis nobler in the mind to suffer" was by rehearsing the material over and over again until you could follow it with "the slings and arrows of outrageous fortune" without looking at the printed text. Thus you continued to activate the same pathways so that changes could take place within them that would serve as the physical manifestation of the memory, which is called an "engram" or "memory trace" by neuroscientists.

The creation of new hippocampal pathways is specific for the information that was repeated and takes time to develop. This is exactly what colleagues and I showed by training rats to learn the location of a hidden platform in a large pool filled with opaque water (i.e., Morris water maze). The animals that were trained to find the platform by learning the location of various landmarks scattered throughout the room showed robust growth of hippocampal axons. However, those animals that merely exercised, which does not require declarative memory formation, didn't show any growth whatsoever in the hippocampus (Holahan, Rekart, Sandoval, & Routtenberg, 2006; Rekart, Sandoval, Bermudez-Rattoni, & Routtenberg, 2007).

Furthermore, we found that at least three days of training (with ten trials per day) were required. Indeed, our results provided a causal mechanism for the observation that in humans the hippocampal volume (both sides) of London cab drivers is larger than that of other individuals (Maguire et al., 2000). The Maguire findings further showed that there was a significant correlation between the size of the hippocampus and driving experience. Those cabbies who had been driving the longest had the largest hippocampi. Thus repeated usage of the hippocampus to store information actually changes the structure of the hippocampus.

It is this ability to modify our brains, the so-called "plasticity" of neural circuitry, that underlies the storage of all declarative memories. As we will see, though repeatedly and persistently activating neural circuitry is a sure-fire way to store declarative memories, there are a number of ways to modify the information so that less activity (i.e., fewer repetitions) will still result in the creation of strong and persistent memory traces.

DISTRIBUTING THE ACTIVITY

When I was an undergraduate student, I was always amazed by the dedication of classmates who were diligent enough to set aside 30 minutes to an hour daily in which to review notes. Those students, not surprisingly, did well on class tests and quizzes. Though I did just fine with my own particular brand of studying, I spent many sleepless nights in the two to three days before an exam catching up on material that I had put off until the "last minute."

Though I never formally kept track, it is a safe bet that over the course of the three weeks between exams, my friends who studied on a regular basis probably studied *less* in terms of overall hours than I did across those two-to-three-day marathon sessions. In effect, I was studying longer but not smarter. If I had only taken the time to go back and review Hermann Ebbinghaus' work from 1885, I would have seen the error of my ways.

Ebbinghaus demonstrated that if he spent a short amount of time every day learning nonsense syllables (though he didn't know it at the time, his choice of nonsense syllables prevented proactive interference — pretty smart), that after just 38 trials spread over three days he would reach perfection. However, when he tried to cram all of the learning into one day it took him almost double (68) the number of repetitions to achieve the same level of accuracy. This finding, that *spaced* (or distributed) learning is better than *massed* (i.e., cramming) has stood the test of time as it holds as true today in the 21st century as it did in the 19th century.

Though Ebbinghaus used three days to learn his syllables, it may be possible to achieve successful encoding with only two days of learning. Some researchers have recently shown that the delay between spaced trials ("gap") may be able to be manipulated so that recollection can be maximized with just two learning sessions (Cepeda, Vul, Rohrer, Wixted, & Pashler, 2008). The gap is the time between the first and second study sessions and the "retention interval" is the time between the second study session and the test. Thus in a class, the gap could be considered the time between the initial lesson and a review session and the retention interval is the time between the review session and the exam.

Laboratory research using foreign language words and simple facts has shown using computer models that the gap that maximizes memory retention occurs when it takes place at a time equivalent to 10–20 percent of the retention interval. At shorter time periods (ten-day retention interval), gap times closer to 10 percent are beneficial (i.e., one day); whereas for longer periods of time, experimental data show that 17 percent may be optimal (i.e., 28-day gap if 168 days will elapse between the second session and the test (Cepeda, Coburn, Rohrer, Wixted, Mozer, & Pashler, 2009).

The good news about implementation of optimal spacing effects in this manner is that it is better to "miss" the optimal date for the second session and have to reschedule it at a later date than to schedule it too early (Cepeda et al., 2009; Pavlik & Anderson, 2008). For example, Carpenter, Pashler, and Cepeda (2009) examined memory in eighth graders who were asked to learn a series of U.S. history facts upon which they were tested nine months later. These authors found that students for whom a gap of 16 weeks was introduced between study sessions remembered more than students with only a one-week gap, even though the optimal gap is probably somewhere between four and six weeks.

In a course that requires long-term retention of factual information, optimal gaps could be used to tailor instruction so that retention is maximized. Though it would certainly be challenging to design an entire curriculum using such gaps (plus, many forms of higher-order information wouldn't lend themselves to this type of training), one can imagine that the judicious placement of such gaps could be used to optimize retention of particularly challenging concepts. Alternatively, they could be used to reduce review time for concepts that are learned early in a semester but that are critical for more advanced concepts that are covered later. Informally, I have designed courses using optimal gaps to maximize retention and reduce review time of particularly challenging concepts (related to the electrophysiological properties of neurons) in 400-level courses in neuroscience and sensation and perception with success.

Of course, in today's classroom, concepts are most often covered for several concurrent days for several reasons, including topical coherence, linearity, and logical structure. And indeed, it should be noted that to date studies on optimal spacing effects, such as those described previously, haven't addressed whether optimal gaps would be useful if they were positioned later in a term.

Thus rather than occurring between stand-alone instructional sessions, study sessions would occur between a block of instruction, encompassing several days to a week and then a review session. Though not research-validated in the strictest sense, it stands to reason that gaps positioned in this manner would be as fruitful, if not more, than those described in the literature.

So how is it that less studying could result in better memory? There are several possible explanations for this. First, we know from the animal literature that time is required for many of the physical changes that underlie learning and memory to become manifest in the brain (e.g., Holahan, Rekart, Sandoval, & Routtenberg, 2006). Second, it is known that our own assessments of how well we know something, which are called "judgments-of-learning" (JOLs) or "metamemory," become more accurate when delays are introduced between study sessions (Nelson & Dunlosky, 1991). The gap may provide time for poorly encoded engrams to disappear, which then allows us to "see" the holes in our own understanding.

Regardless of the mechanism, what isn't disputed is that so-called "overlearning," or continuing to study even though mastery has been truly achieved, does not necessarily result in enhanced retention (Rohrer, Taylor, Pashler, Wixted, & Cepeda, 2005).

HOW WE THINK ABOUT WHAT IS TO BE LEARNED

Though as we have just seen that the interval between lectures and reviews can greatly affect how well information is remembered, we have yet to discuss how the ways in which we think about the stimuli themselves can influence encoding.

To illustrate this point, we are going to do two quick demonstrations. First, read each word in List 1. After you have read a word, you need to next think about how many letters are present in that word before moving on to the next word in the list. Finally, after you have thought about the number of letters in the last word in the list, I would like you to look away (or cover it up) from the list and count down from 30 (this works best if you do it out loud—really). Once you have finished the countdown, please write down all of the words that you can remember.

LIST 1: boy tank tulip tuba whip swing honey lunch nail notch lark

For the second list, you will read each word and then you will need to visualize what the noun form of the word actually looks like. Then you can move on to the next word. As before, after you have imagined what the last word looks like, count down (out loud) from 30 and then write down as many words as you can. Good luck.

LIST 2: angel drip pillow spoon horse song bee toast house dirt girl

Now that you are done with both lists, you need to compare the answers with the original words that were presented. Cross out any words that you "remembered" that weren't actually on the lists and then count up the total number correct. Chances are great that in comparing the two lists, you remembered two or more words from the second list than you did from the first.

These findings, which exploit what are called *levels of processing*, are similar to those first described by Craik and Tulving in 1975. The reason why the second list is better remembered is because during encoding you had to engage in what is called *deep* processing. Deeply processed information is better remembered than shallow processed information (like counting the number of letters) because of greater and more extensive activation of the brain during encoding (Kapur et al., 1994).

The effect of the level of processing upon encoding is an important one. Indeed, this effect is one reason why I encourage my students to do away with highlighters. Highlighters give students the false impression that studying is taking place. In the end, the amount of time spent reading over the specific words or concepts to be highlighted is probably equal to or less than the amount of time just devoted to counting the number of letters in words.

I recommend that my students take the few seconds that they would normally highlight a passage and use it to visualize and think about what they have read. Not only will this momentary visualization of the material assist with encoding due to greater brain activation (relative to the simplistic motor task of moving the marker over the page), it may also help to identify what is not known or is unclear, thus engaging metamemory processes.

Chapter 5

Sometimes the properties of the stimuli themselves determine how well they will be remembered. Think about the last time you were in a city—and for this exercise the larger the city, the better. Do any particular individuals, not friends or family or work acquaintances but *strangers*, come to mind? Are there people whom you've never actually met that you can remember from your time in a large metropolitan area, such as Chicago or Boston? If the answer is "yes," then think about the properties of that individual that are so memorable. Was s/he wearing something unusual? Perhaps it was obvious that s/he had fallen on some hard times and was perhaps homeless? Or maybe, you saw someone who enjoys some degree of celebrity or fame?

Regardless of the specifics of the person, what needs to be considered is what sets that person apart from any of the other individuals whose paths also crossed yours. Indeed, a city setting is most illustrative because it is likely that while in a city, dozens, if not hundreds, of people walked by you. Though you most likely saw each one, you encoded few, if any, of them and thus have no recollection of what they looked like.

The chances are excellent that the person or few people whom you actually do remember had something about them that was *distinct*. You likely didn't set out to remember this individual, but their *distinctiveness*, the property that literally made them stand out in a crowd, facilitated your encoding of them. Distinctiveness operates on a neural level that, unlike the levels of processing just discussed, doesn't require our conscious control. There is no reason for you to want to remember a few strangers, yet you do anyway.

Though the example just given tapped into episodic memories, distinctiveness also affects the storage of semantic information. The following example is another one of our fantastic word lists. Read through the entire list once, then take a 30-second break and do something to distract yourself to avoid conscious rehearsal (i.e., use of your phonoarticulatory loop). I find that just counting down from 30 out loud works well.

I also like to "spice up" the rather mundane activity by adding a particular flair to the last ten seconds, akin to the launch of a rocket. Alternatively, I also recite some of the countdown as though I were in Barcelona and count in Spanish. Once the 30 seconds have elapsed, write down all of the words that you can recall. Ready:

WORD	DOOR	DESK	MONITOR	CORD	MUG
TAPE	CLIP	PAPER	OUTLET	WINDOW	FAN
CABINET	LIGHT	FILE	UNICORN	SPEAKER	GLOBE
BINDER	FRAME	LOCK	CUSHION	FRAME	CHAIR

Now compare your list with the one provided and cross out any words that you remembered but shouldn't have.

For our purposes here, the exact number of words that you remember isn't a factor but rather which words you recalled. As probably was abundantly clear as you read through the list (and as the song goes), one of those things was not like the others. Though most of the words were rather bland and commonplace, "UNICORN," likely stood out and was one of the six to ten words from the list of 20 that you remembered. The conceptual or semantic distinctiveness of words thus influences their encoding and subsequent retrieval (e.g., Hunt & Mitchell, 1982). If instead of office equipment and supplies, our list consisted of words like "OGRE," "FAIRY," "DRAGON," and so forth, then the word "UNICORN" would no longer be preferentially encoded.

Stimuli that are unusual or distinct may be remembered better in relation to relatively mundane information. This memory-enhancing effect can be put to good use in a classroom. Often times in my classes, I will use bizarre or seemingly out-of-place examples in order to facilitate learning on the part of my students. Once I used the example of a wolverine (the small, woodland mammal, not the mascot of a Big Ten school or the Marvel superhero) ambushing a student in the parking lot to illustrate the physiology of the stress response (don't worry, no real students were harmed during the story).

Though the wolverine itself had nothing to do with the actual concepts that I was discussing about the release of hormones and neurotransmitters, I have little doubt that the bizarreness of the story, which I must admit that I acted out with great flair, did influence the encoding of the information that I actually wanted my students to learn (e.g., McDaniel & Einstein, 1986).

Indeed, when grading essay tests that assessed recall and application of the concepts related to this stress phenomenon, I noted that several students wrote the word "wolverine" in the margin of their paper, most likely as a mnemonic aid that helped them to organize their thoughts. All of the students who in some way referenced the "wolverine" earned full credit for the question.

Why do distinctive items enjoy preferential treatment when it comes to encoding? The answer isn't entirely clear. Though attention may play a role, it isn't the whole story. Likely there is an activation of a greater number or a more widespread network of brain connections when we encounter something that isn't quite right—contextual *non sequiturs*. If this is the case, then it may be that the difficulty of processing the stimuli is what contributes to their successful encoding. Learning which is more difficult, as may occur with distinct items, may engender greater learning. Indeed, this is exactly what has been shown to occur.

This phenomenon, sometimes referred to as *cognitive disfluency*, has been shown to positively affect the encoding and retrieval of information. Diemand-Yauman, Oppenheimer, and Vaughn (2010) showed how a subtle manipulation of the format in which information is presented can have lasting and pronounced effects on memory encoding. In the laboratory, they presented information about three hypothetical alien species (to avoid any effects of prior learning) to participants with a normal font (16-point, Arial) or one of two modified fonts that were (1) smaller (12-point font), (2) in gray rather than black, and (3) were less commonly used fonts in educational settings: the informal Comic Sans (which resembles the writing used in the credits of the animated television series, *The Simpsons*) or the somewhat fancy Bodoni MT.

After the information was presented, memory was assessed 15 minutes later. The researchers found that though there were no differences between the two unusual fonts, participants who read the descriptions of the aliens using those fonts remembered significantly more (13.7%) than the students who were given the standard font. Given the pronounced differences that were seen in the laboratory, the researchers then validated their results in a high school setting.

In their second study, they changed only the fonts (e.g., didn't adjust grayscale) of PowerPoints and worksheets for six different courses, ranging from AP physics to history, throughout an entire semester. Just as with the laboratory, they found that overall individuals who were presented with the odd fonts (no difference between three fonts that were used: Haettenschweiler, *Comic Sans* [italicized], or Monotype Corsiva) that were designed to produce disfluency did best on course-embedded assessments throughout the semester. Thus even something as simple as modifying the font that is used during instruction can positively influence encoding.

ENHANCING ENCODING THROUGH EMOTION

Though common lore dictates that emotions cloud logic, the same is not true for memory. Indeed, on a personal level emotion is responsible for the encoding of some of our most revered memories. The types of episodic memories we most often recall are those that were chock-full of emotion at the time of encoding. Our episodic memories are a collection of "firsts" (e.g., first day of school, first kiss, first time driving alone). When they first happened, these events likely contained a mixture of emotional feelings, including apprehension and excitement.

The facilitating effect of emotion on memory can be put to good use in the classroom where emotion can also influence the ways in which we encode information for the better. Before beginning to address exactly how emotion can be used to enhance memory and understanding, let's look at how an emotion sends the message to the brain to "record."

An emotion is a physiological and cognitive response to some form of stimulus. The stimulus can be either internal (i.e., a thought) or external. For the sake of simplicity, let's focus on an external stimulus in the anecdote that follows. When my family and I moved into our there were some large rocks in our yard that needed t moved many of these rocks without incident; however, rock that made a lasting impression upon me. This parti large, not the largest that I had to transfer to another location but large enough that I had to use a shovel to pry it up and over into a wheelbarrow that I was using.

As I lifted up the rock high enough to get a hand under it, a black and yellow snake about a foot in length came slithering out from under the rock where it had been sleeping. I was immediately startled and dropped the rock (don't worry . . . the snake made it out just fine). Now despite the fact that I must have moved dozens of rocks that day, why is this the only rock I that I actually remember via my episodic memory?

After I lifted the rock and saw the snake, my eyes sensed the visual characteristics of the snake which it sent to my brain. My brain then identified the snake as a threat by matching it to examples within my mind of known threats. Once recognized, signals were sent to my amygdala, which is responsible for my processing of emotional stimuli, particularly those high in arousal. The amygdala, in turn, then activated my hippocampus, and in effect told it "this is important, we will need to remember this." This is why to this day I can still picture not only the snake but the rock under which it was sleeping. As we will see in our discussion of retrieval, when the threat response is long-lived (i.e., as with stress), the amygdala also activates the hypothalamus, which activates the pituitary gland, which in turn signals the release of adrenaline and cortisol from the adrenal glands (Herman & Cullinan, 1997).

My assertion that I remember one rock out of dozens because my amygdala was activated by the snake unexpectedly slithering towards me is supported by a wealth of laboratory studies. In a series of classic studies, Drs. James McGaugh, Larry Cahill, and colleagues examined whether emotion could be used to enhance the encoding of stimuli that didn't themselves pose a threat. In one study, they used 12 slides that depicted a story wherein a boy and his mother cross a street en route to visit the father at a hospital, there are some wrecked cars, and, finally, there are scenes from a hospital (Cahill & McGaugh, 1995).

The researchers randomly assigned college-aged students to one of two groups: neutral captions or emotional captions. In the neutral caption group, the participants read about how the boy and his mother crossed the street, saw some wrecked cars, and then visited his father at the hospital, where the staff were undergoing a disaster drill. In the emotional caption group, the participants read about how the boy was struck by a car as he was crossing the street and how he suffered critical injuries, including head trauma and having his feet severed.

What is important about this study is that for the first four slides (boy and his mother going to visit dad), the captions and the pictures were the me in both groups. For the next eight slides, though the captions differed between the two groups (emotion = car accident involving boy; neutral = disaster drill) all of the pictures seen were the same. On a subsequent test of memory, the recall of events on the first four slides was no different between the two groups. However, those who read the emotional captions got an average of 15 percent more of the details correct when tested on material coincident with the onset of the emotional captions (slides five through eight). Thus, even though the participants weren't in any harm and the captions didn't depict anything that really happened, the emotionally charged information was better remembered.

Importantly, the same research group also examined whether a drug known to inhibit the responsiveness of the amygdala, a so-called "beta blocker" (propranolol hydrochloride), which has been used to treat anxiety, would impair memory. Though it had no effect on the memory for non-emotional details, it significantly blocked the enhancing effects of emotion.

Participants who received this drug and who were in the emotional group did no better than those in the neutral condition (Cahil, Prins, Weber, & McGaugh, 1994). These researchers further confirmed the role of the amygdala when they demonstrated a striking relationship between the level of memory for emotional films and the amount of amygdala activation observed (using PET) while the participants first watched the films three weeks prior (Cahill, Haier, Fallon, Alkire, Tang, Keator, Wu, & McGaugh, 1996).

So how can all of this knowledge about emotion be put to use in a classroom? First, we must recognize that all stimuli in our environment have an inherent valence (pleasantness/unpleasantness) and level of arousal (which affects whether we are physiologically excited) associated with them. Though a picture of a house is neutral and of negligible arousal, an image of a house on fire is both negative and high in arousal. Words act the same way. Though many words are neutral (e.g., the word "item"), others, such as "lightning," are high in arousal.

Though you may feel as though our responses to words are completely subjective, when asked to rate how the words make them feel, most people rate words similarly on these two dimensions (Bradley & Lang, 1999). Thus it is possible to enhance memory by using emotionally charged words.

Now, to this point all of the studies that we have discussed on emotion and memory have used high-arousal, negatively valenced stimuli. Given that feelings of safety are of paramount importance in a classroom, it is good to know that positive and negative words are remembered equally well so long as they are high in arousal (e.g., Doerksen & Shimamura, 2001). Why does arousal have to be high? Because arousal refers to a physiological change in the way we feel when we are exposed to the stimulus (in this case, the word). This physiological change is necessary to activate the amygdala.

Once the amygdala has been activated, its modulation of the hippocampus results in an increased ability to store information. Thus the words that are used in a classroom when talking about various phenomena may make more of a difference than the average educator believes. A list of potentially high-arousing, positively valenced nouns that could be used in the classroom is found in the following:

TRIUMPH	HOLIDAY	BIRTHDAY	CARNIVAL
CHEER	SURPRISE	CIRCUS	ROLLER COASTER
VICTORY	PARTY	FESTIVAL	SKYDIVING
REWARD	TREASURE	PRIZE	ADVENTURE
SAFARI	MISSION		

The words from that list could be used in any number of different ways; for example, to enhance learning of new adjectives or as background to an anecdote that makes a point or teaches a particular concept. What should be kept in mind is that the list is by no means exhaustive but rather gives a sampling of what high-arousal, pleasant words *look like* so that others you can think of could be used.

The words themselves are being used in this context to activate the amygdala to store information. Whether used in mathematical word problems or as modifiers (or what is modified) by new spelling words, there is no reason *not* to use these types of stimuli to increase students' physiological arousal. It doesn't matter that the words themselves aren't of interest to the educator because they will still influence the memory of the other stimuli associated with them (Doerksen & Shimamura, 2001). In addition, pictures that are high in positive arousal have been shown to have the same effect (e.g., Anderson, Wais, & Gabrieli, 2006).

Furthermore, advantages may be conferred by increasing the general level of physiological arousal in the classroom. Humor and laughter likely increase physiological arousal (Martin, 2001). It stands to reason that humorous material may be better remembered than non-humorous. In fact, there is an enhancement for the free recall of humorous sentences (Schmidt, 1994) and humorous puns (Lippman & Dunn, 2000; Summerfelt, Lippman, & Hyman, 2010) relative to non-humorous sentences. Thus using funny or laughter-inducing examples may also facilitate learning.

Though it isn't entirely clear whether the memory-enhancing effects of humor are due to arousal alone or a combination of arousal and the increased attention that is triggered by humor (Schmidt, 1994), all that matters is that laughter is a safe and enjoyable way to appropriately increase the arousal level of an entire class.

POINTS TO REMEMBER:

- Long-term memory can be divided into two main types: declarative and non-declarative.
- Declarative memory consists of memory for facts (semantic) and actual experiences that we can remember in detail (episodic).
- The first stage of memory is called encoding, which is the same thing as learning. After information has been encoded, it is next stored. Finally, memories are retrieved when the information that is stored is needed.
- Memories are stored in brain regions, such as the hippocampus, that are critical for long-term declarative memories, through modifications to existing neural connections.
- Information is learned best when learning is distributed over time.
- Long-term learning can be maximized by having a study session take place at an interval that is 10–20 percent of the time between the study session and the exam.
- Deep learning is facilitated by thinking deeply about information. This strategy can be instituted merely by visualizing what is to be remembered.
- Information that is novel or distinct will be remembered better than information that is more day-to-day.
- Increasing the difficulty of learning enhances memory. This can be achieved simply by using out-of-the-ordinary fonts that are slightly harder to read.
- Physiological arousal enhances memory encoding. Increases in physiological arousal can be safely achieved using words, images, and other stimuli known to evoke heightened levels of arousal.
- Humor and laugher may be effective strategies for increasing the general level of arousal in a classroom.

NOTES

1. Though other researchers use the terms "explicit" and "implicit" in place of "declarative" and "non-declarative," respectively (e.g., Tulving), we will use the latter terms as they more readily describe the differences between the two broad categories.

2. Though Hollywood has produced a number of movies with poorly conceived and inaccurate depictions of amnesia, the 2000 film "Memento," written and directed by Christopher Nolan, does a good job of trying to capture the horrors of anterograde amnesia.

REFERENCES

Adams, P. (1998). Hebb and Darwin. *Journal of Theoretical Biology*, 195(4), 419–438.

Anderson, A. K., Wais, P. E., & Gabrieli, J. D. E. (2006). Emotion enhances remembrance of neutral events past. *Proceedings of the National Academy of Sciences, U.S.A., 103*, 1599–1604.

Blumenfeld, R.S. & Ranganath, C. (2007). Prefrontal cortex and long-term memory encoding: An integrative review of findings from neuropsychology and neuroimaging. *The Neuroscientist, 13*(3), 280-291.

Bradley, M. M., & Lang, P. J. (1999). *International affective digitized sounds (IADS): Stimuli, instruction manual and affective ratings* (Tech. Rep. No. B-2). Gainesville, FL: The Center for Research in Psychophysiology, University of Florida.

Brewer, J. B., Zhao, Z., Desmond, J. E., Glover, G. H., & Gabrieli, J. D. E. (1998). Making memories: Brain activity that predicts how well visual experience will be remembered. *Science, 281,* 1185–1187.

Buckner, R. L., Kelley, W. M., & Petersen, S. E. (1999). Frontal cortex contributes to human memory formation. *Nature Neuroscience, 2*(4), 311–314.

Cahill, L., Prins, B., Weber, M., & McGaugh, J. L. (1994). β-Adrenergic activation and memory for emotional events. *Nature, 371,* 702–704.

Cahill, L., & McGaugh, J. L. (1995). A novel demonstration of enhanced memory associated with emotional arousal. *Consciousness and Cognition, 4,* 410–421.

Cahill, L., Haier, T. R. J., Fallon, J., Alkire, M. T., Tang, C., Keaton, D., Wu, J., & McGaugh, J. L. (1996). Amygdala activity at encoding correlated with long-term, free recall of emotional information. *Proceedings of the National Academy of Sciences, U.S.A., 93,* 8016–8021.

Carpenter, S. K., Pashler, H., & Cepeda, N. J. (2009). Using tests to enhance 8th grade students' retention of U. S. history facts. *Applied Cognitive Psychology, 23,* 760-771.

Cepeda, N. J., Vul, E., Rohrer, D., Wixted, J. T., & Pashler, H. (2008). Spacing effects in learning: A temporal ridgeline of optimal retention. *Psychological Science, 19*(11), 1095–1102.

Cepeda, N. J., Coburn, N., Rohrer, D., Wixted, J. T., Mozer, M. C., & Pashler, H. (2009). Optimizing distributed practice: Theoretical analysis and practical implications. *Experimental Psychology, 56*(4), 236–246.

Corkin, S. (2002). What's new with the amnesic patient H. M.? *Nature Reviews Neuroscience, 3*(2), 153–160.

Craik, F. I. M., & Tulving, E. (1975). Depth of processing and the retention of words in episodic memory. *Journal of Experimental Psychology: General, 104*(3), 268–294.

Diemand-Yauman, C., Oppenheimer, D. M., & Vaughan, E. B. (2010). Fortune favors the bold (and the italicized): Effects of disfluency on educational outcomes. *Cognition, 118*(1), 111–115.

Doerksen, S., & Shimamura, A. P. (2001). Source memory enhancement for emotional words. *Emotion, 1*(1), 5–11.

Ebbinghaus, H. (1885/1913). *Memory. A Contribution to Experimental Psychology*. New York: Teachers College, Columbia University.

Fell, J., Klaver, P., Lehnertz, K., Grunwald, T., Schaller, C., Elger, & C. E., Fernández, G. (2001). Human memory formation is accompanied by rhinal-hippocampal coupling and decoupling. *Nature Neuroscience, 4*(12), 1259–1264.

Fell, J., Ludowig, E., Rosburg, T., Axmacher, N., & Elger, C. E. (2008). Phase-locking within the human mediotemporal lobe predicts memory formation. *Neuroimage, 43*(2), 410–419.

Goswami, U. (2006). Neuroscience and education: From research to practice? *Nature Reviews Neuroscience, 7,* 406–411.

Habib, R., Nyberg, L., & Tulving, E. (2003). Hemispheric asymmetries of memory: The HERA model revisited. *Trends in Cognitive Science, 7*(6), 241–245.

Hebb, D. O. (1949). *The organization of behavior: A neuropsychological theory*. New York: John Wiley and Sons.

Herman, J. P., & Cullinan, W. E. (1997). Neurocircuitry of stress: Central control of the hypothalamo–pituitary–adrenocortical axis. *Trends in Neurosciences, 20*(2), 78–84.

Holahan, M., Rekart, J. L., Sandoval, J., & Routtenberg, A. (2006). Spatial learning induces presynaptic structural remodeling in the hippocampal mossy fiber system of two rat strains. *Hippocampus 16*(6), 560–570.
Hunt, R. R., & Mitchell, D. B. (1982). Independent effects of semantic and nonsemantic distinctiveness. *Journal of Experimental Psychology: Learning, Memory, and Cognition, 8*(1), 81–87.
Kapur, S., Craik, F. I. M., Tulving, E., Wilson, A. A., Houle, S., & Brown, G. M. (1994). Neuroanatomical correlates of encoding in episodic memory: Levels of processing effect. *Proceedings of the National Academy of Sciences, U.S.A., 91*, 2008–2011.
Kelley, W. M., Miezin, F. M., McDermott, K. B., Buckner, R. L., Raichle, M. E., Cohen, N. J., Ollinger, J. M., Akbudak, E., Conturo, T. E., Snyder, A. Z., & Petersen, S. E. (1998). Hemispheric specialization in human dorsal frontal cortex and medial temporal lobe for verbal and nonverbal memory encoding. *Neuron, 20*, 927–936.
Lippman, L. G., & Dunn, M. L. (2000). Contextual connections within puns: Effects on perceived humor and memory. *The Journal of General Psychology, 127*(2), 185–197.
Maguire, E. A., Gadian, D. G., Johnsrude, I. S., Good, C. D., Ashburner, J., Frackowiak, R. S. J., & Frith, C.D. (2000). Navigation-related structural change in the hippocampi of taxi drivers. *Proceedings of the National Academy of Sciences, 97*(8), 4398–4403.
Martin, R. A. (2001). Humor, laughter, and physical health: Methodological issues and research findings. *Psychological Bulletin, 127*(4), 504–519.
McDaniel, M. A., & Einstein, G. O. (1986). Bizarre imagery as an effective memory aid: The importance of distinctiveness. *Journal of Experimental Psychology: Learning, Memory, and Cognition, 12*, 54–65.
Nelson, T. O., & Dunlosky, J. (1991). When people's judgments of learning (JOLs) are extremely accurate at predicting subsequent recall: The "delayed-JOL effect." *Psychological Science, 2*(4), 267–270.
Pavlik, P. I., & Anderson, J. R. (2008). Using a model to compute the optimal schedule of practice. *Journal of Experimental Psychology: Applied, 14*(2), 101–117.
Penfield, W. (1958). Some mechanisms of consciousness discovered during electrical stimulation of the brain. *Proceedings of the National Academy of Sciences, U.S.A., 44*(2), 51–66.
Ramón y Cajal, S. (1911/1995). *Histology of the nervous system*. Translated by Neely Swanson and Larry W. Swanson. *History of neuroscience*. New York: Oxford University Press.
Rekart, J. L., Sandoval, J., Bermudez-Rattoni, F., and Routtenberg, A. (2007). Remodeling of hippocampal mossy fibers is selectively induced seven days after the acquisition of a spatial but not a cued reference memory task. *Learning & Memory, 14*(6), 416–421.
Rekart, J. L., & Routtenberg, A. (2008). Post-translational brain protein modification as substrate for memories that last a lifetime. *BioTech International. 20*(5), 6–8.
Rohrer, D., Taylor, K., Pashler, H., Wixted, J. T., & Cepeda, N. J. (2005). The effect of overlearning on long-term retention. *Applied Cognitive Psychology, 19*, 361–374.
Schmidt, S. R. (1994). Effects of humor on sentence memory. *Journal of Experimental Psychology: Learning, Memory, and Cognition, 20*(4), 953–967.
Scoville, W. B., & Milner, B. (1957). Loss of recent memory after bilateral hippocampal lesions. *Journal of Neurology, Neurosurgery & Psychiatry, 20*(1), 11–21.
Small, S. A., Nava, A. S., Perrera, G. M., DeLaPaz, R., Mayeux, R., & Stern. Y. (2001). Circuit mechanisms underlying memory encoding and retrieval in the long axis of the hippocampal formation. *Nature Neuroscience, 4*(4), 442–449.
Squire, L. R., & Zola, S. M. (1996). The structure and function of declarative and nondeclarative memory systems. *Proceedings of the National Academy of Sciences, USA, 93*, 13515–13522.
Summerfelt, H., Lippman, L., & Hyman, Jr., I. E. (2010). The effect of humor on memory: Constrained by the pun. *The Journal of General Psychology, 137*(4), 376–394.

SIX
Long-term Memory Retrieval

Stored information is only useful if it can be retrieved when needed. As anyone who has ever struggled on a question on an exam knows, this isn't always the case. Why is it that sometimes we just *know* that we studied something but can't quite seem to recall what *it* was? What tricks can we use to facilitate the retrieval of information, and is it possible to use retrieval mechanisms to actually enhance encoding? This chapter will answer these questions.

RETRIEVAL AND THE BRAIN

The brain utilizes many of the same structures involved in the encoding of long-term declarative information (again, hereafter referred to solely as *memory*) for the retrieval of memories. According to the HERA model (Tulving, Kapur, Craik, Moscovitch, & Houle, 1994), regions of the right frontal lobe of the brain are preferentially activated for the retrieval of episodic memories (remember that the left frontal lobe is activated during encoding).

The hippocampus and other medial temporal lobe structures are also used for retrieval. Remember our discussion of the patient H. M. who had both of his hippocampi removed to treat seizures (i.e., chapter 5)? Though the most debilitating feature of his memory deficit was his anterograde amnesia (his inability to store new long-term information), that wasn't the only form of amnesia that his surgical removal of his hippocampi caused. H. M. also had mild *retrograde* amnesia, which is an inability to remember events from one's past (Corkin, 2002).

H. M.'s retrograde amnesia was fairly pronounced for events that took place in the three years immediately preceding his surgery; however, for most older events, his memory was perfect. He could recall, with great detail, many aspects of his childhood, his use of language and command of facts was largely intact, and his I.Q. even *rose* slightly after the surgery.

Why would H. M. also lose the ability to retrieve some older memories as well as store new ones? The answer lies with the structure that was removed. The hippocampus is believed to be responsible for the transfer of information from short-term memory stores to areas of the brain that have the ability to hold information indefinitely. There are many hypotheses related to exactly how the hippocampus does this, though most have the idea of *organization* in common.

The hippocampus is responsible for binding together previously unconnected engrams within the brain so that memory is cohesive. As we'll see, this process, sometimes referred to as *elaboration*, then makes it easier to retrieve a memory, even when only a few aspects of it are present.

For example, have you ever been walking in the autumn and the aroma of wet leaves (if you live in a temperate climate) brought back a vivid episodic memory from when you were in school? Or a perfume or cologne reminded you instantly of someone whom you hadn't thought of in years? These are examples of how one component of a memory, in this case a smell (which is the sense most associated with emotional memories), can evoke an entire episode from memory. Though the memory actually consists of many experiences, including sights and sounds and feelings, only one portion of it (a *cue*) is necessary to trigger retrieval and reminiscence.

Though the actual engrams for the various components of the memory are likely distributed throughout the cortex, the hippocampus seems to remain involved in linking together some information for at least a few years after the event has taken place. Over time, connections between cortical areas eventually strengthen (with repeated and persistent activation per Hebb; see chapter 5) and memories are able to be evoked without the intervention of the hippocampus. Thus the removal of the hippocampus takes with it the ability to access relatively recent memories that haven't been sufficiently *consolidated* (which is the process via which a memory becomes relatively immune to disruption).

This transient dependence on the hippocampus is related to the ease with which memories may be disrupted and/or destroyed. Our old friend, the father of modern memory research, Hermann Ebbinghaus (1885), was the first to show that the amount of information we can recall declines precipitously, from almost 100 percent immediately to no more than 20 percent after six hours (provided that we haven't used rehearsal mechanisms or any of the cognitive tips that were covered in the last chapter). This forgetting curve is directly related to consolidation.

Using rodents, Carl Duncan (1949) showed that the susceptibility of a memory to destruction or disruption closely follows the forgetting curve of Ebbinghaus. Our newest and most recent memories are the most susceptible to disruption (Duncan used mild electrical shock to demonstrate this). Duncan's findings have been subsequently demonstrated by others, who have demonstrated that the same timeline is seen in humans undergoing electroconvulsive therapy (ECT; Squire, Slater, & Chace, 1975).

Over time, as memories become consolidated, they are elaborated sufficiently that they can withstand most minor assaults. Major assaults, such as the neurodegeneration that occurs with Alzheimer's disease, also result in the same pattern of amnesia: those memories that are the oldest are the last to wither and disappear. The strength of memories, as demonstrated by forgetting curves and the graded nature of retrograde amnesia, is a direct result of the elaboration of memories.

The oldest memories reside in engrams that (1) have the most connections, (2) are strongly connected to one another, and (3) are widely distributed. This is what makes them so persistent. In fact, what we think of as our oldest memories are really our most distributed. Put differently, long-term memory is a byproduct of space and not time *per se* (Rekart & Routtenberg, 2008).

SEMANTIC ORGANIZATION AND RETRIEVAL

As a brief demonstration of retrieval processes, let's try to remember some capitals of countries. Look at the list below and try, using only your memory, to name the capital of each nation:

SWITZERLAND
ICELAND
DENMARK
CANADA
AUSTRALIA

If you were unable to remember any (and to make sure that you are accurate), I'll give you the first letter of each country's capital as a hint:

SWITZERLAND: B_____
ICELAND: R_____
DENMARK: C_____
CANADA: O_____
AUSTRALIA: C_____

If the hint helped you at all (or caused you to reconsider a capital), then you have experienced what is known as a tip-of-the-tongue phenomenon (Brown & McNeill, 1966). This phenomenon occurs when we have difficulty retrieving a memory that we know that we have. One of the best ways to locate the "lost" memory is by going through the alphabet letter by letter. In the previous example, I bypassed this and provided the alphabetic hints for you. If the hints (or your memory) worked, then you would have written:

SWITZERLAND: BERN
ICELAND: REYKJAVIK
DENMARK: COPENHAGEN
CANADA: OTTAWA
AUSTRALIA: CANBERRA

The fact that alphabetic hints can help retrieve memories provides insight into the ways that they are stored. Verbal information is likely stored, in part, based on the actual phonological code (which often times is closely related to the spelling). The linking of new information with older, previously stored memories is the elaboration process mentioned earlier in the chapter. Elaborative processes are important because they facilitate efficient and expedient retrieval of information. They also allow for remembrance to take place with what is called a *partial cue*, meaning only a subset of the original information.

The initial letters of national capitals are partial verbal cues because all of the orthographic information (i.e., the spelling of the word) wasn't provided. Thus, with verbal information, the spelling, the phonetics, as well as the meaning of words are important cues for retrieval.

How we store verbal memory, within so-called semantic networks, is of particular importance to cognitive psychologists. Indeed, despite the fact that each of us has had a widely different set of experiences in our lives, we actually store information in strikingly similar ways and locations within our brains. For example, for each of the words that follow, please write down the first corresponding object that comes to mind. Focus on the broad way that you would identify the object rather than the specific. Thus if the category word listed were "VEHICLE," you would write down "CAR" or "TRUCK" but not "Ford Ranger." Let's give it a try:

CLOTHING
FURNITURE
WEAPON
FRUIT

Chances are good that you wrote down the following words for each of the broad categories listed. For "CLOTHING," you most likely thought of either "pants" (or jeans) or "shirt" and for furniture a "sofa" or "couch." There is almost no doubt that for the third category, the word "gun" was retrieved (which says something about society in general, but that is for a different discussion). The last category, "FRUIT," is a little trickier. If you are from North of the Mason-Dixon line, "apple" may have been what you wrote; if you are from the South or California, then "orange" is slightly more likely.

So how am I able to predict these categories with a fairly high degree of success (at least three out of four for most readers)? My predictions are based on the results of a study that asked participants to do exactly what you were asked to do: just think of the first, general category of item that comes to mind. It doesn't matter that the actual study took place in 1975 (a particularly good year) or that the participants in question were undergraduate students at Stanford University (Rosch & Mervis, 1975).

Despite the many differences between those of us alive now and those who participated in this study, I knew that we semantically organize information in very similar ways. The first item that comes to mind is an exemplar, that item which best typifies the category. Socially or geographically, there aren't any real differences between people in the United States based on clothing, furniture, or, unfortunately, weapons.

The category "FRUIT," however, does have a bit of a geographic dependence. This is based on the fact that our memories, within so-called superordinate categories (i.e., the broadest way that something can be classified), are arranged around *exemplars*. Exemplars are those items that are most typical or best capture the qualities of the category. Thus, for us in the 21st century, the exemplar of "VEHICLE" (which appeared in the original study) would still be "car" or "truck," just as it was over a quarter of a century ago. Similarly, if you were raised in Southern California or Florida, then oranges and other citrus fruit, which are readily available, and not apples, may be the exemplars for you.

One can hypothesize that if the ways that we as people classify information are the same, then the brain locations and structures underlying those memories must also be similar. Indeed, imaging studies have shown that our brains segregate information within the brain in a structured manner based on whether an item is alive or not, and even whether it is an animal or a human (Damasio et al., 1996). Thus the conceptual properties of information help to determine exactly where new data will be stored within the overarching semantic networks of our memories.

Within the brain, categories (e.g., "animal" or "tool") provide landmarks that direct the storage of information. This organization facilitates rapid retrieval, so that when you see a large, four-legged mammal with a mane you know right away that it is a horse. If, however, you encounter something that is confusing, it makes it difficult to know where to file the information. If it is difficult to file, it is equally difficult to retrieve.

To this end, it makes sense for teachers to assist with the semantic filing of information within student brains. There are a number of techniques already in place that can assist in this way, such as concept maps or outlines. By challenging students to organize information, it should force new concepts into appropriate loci within the broader semantic network and thus facilitate retrieval.

The key is for memory to be able to be retrieved by just the right number and complement of cues (i.e., information associated with parts of the memory). Interestingly, most of the cues that are present at the time of learning can act to trigger later retrieval for the memory. For example, even the physical location where learning takes place (e.g., the classroom) can be considered a cue (Smith, Glenberg, & Bjork, 1978).

When I was an undergraduate at Indiana University, midterm and final examinations were given concurrently to all students in high enrollment classes such as General Chemistry. Though most, if not all, of the lecture classes took place at varying times of the day, the examinations took place at night and most often in different rooms in different buildings on campus. Thus, though I sat through lectures in the Harry G. Day Lecture Hall in the Chemistry Building from 8:00 a.m. to 8:50 a.m. three days a week, I might have to take my midterm in Ballantine Hall and my final in Woodburn—both at 6:30 at night.

Unfortunately for me and the other students, our professors didn't realize that students who are able to take an exam in the same room in which they received instruction do significantly better (Van Der Wege & Barry, 2008). Why? Because the room has contextual cues that can be used to retrieve memories.

TESTING, RETRIEVAL, AND MEMORY ENHANCEMENT

Given the fervor surrounding so-called "high stakes" testing in the United States, is there reason to believe that any form of testing is beneficial to students? Put differently, are tests and quizzes actually pedagogical tools or just forms of assessment used to identify and sort students into various tiers? Research demonstrates the utility of testing for long-term student learning with great clarity.

In a set of elegantly designed studies, cognitive psychologist Dr. Henry Roediger and colleagues directly compared the short- and long-term effects of testing upon student recall of learned facts. One study exposed groups of university students to prose passages that were rich with information about a particular topic (e.g., sea otters). The students then were randomly assigned to one of three groups.

Group one read the passage for a total of 20 minutes split into four 5-minute study sessions (group "SSSS" where each "S" represents a study session) separated by two-minute intervals of unrelated math problems (i.e., a distractor task). Group two studied the passage for three 5-minute periods and then was asked to recall everything known about the passage from memory during a ten-minute "test" period (group "SSST," with the "T" representing the final "test" period). Finally, the third group read the passage for only one 5-minute period, after which students engaged in three testing sessions (group "STTT").

It should be noted that no feedback was given after the "test" sessions; thus, students in the STTT group didn't know whether they were recalling accurate information on subsequent tests (i.e., the second or third testing session; Roediger and Karpicke, 2006).

When memory for the prose passages was assessed one week later, a striking pattern was found. Participants in the STTT group remembered 21 percent more facts from the passage than participants in the SSSS group. In addition, the participants with only one test session, the SSST group, had recall that closely resembled that of the well-performing STTT group (SSST remembered 5 percent less) and still remembered 15 percent more than the SSSS group.

These findings clearly demonstrate that studying more isn't necessarily the key to academic success. Indeed, the participants in the SSSS group actually read the passage, on average, approximately four times more than participants in the STTT group (Roediger & Karpicke, 2006). The amount of studying likely led the SSSS group to feel good about their knowledge. When participants were asked how much they felt they would remember in a week's time after they completed their study and/or test sessions, the SSSS group was significantly more confident than the STTT group. Thus judgments-of-learning weren't successful predictors of future success (Roediger & Karpicke, 2006). So, why did the testing groups do so much better?

Though not known for certain, it may be that a number of processes mediate what is known as *test-enhanced learning*. First, what is known as transfer-appropriate processing (TAP) may be at work (Morris, Bransford, & Francks, 1977). Transfer-appropriate processing suggests that memory is best recalled when it is stored in a format that closely resembles how it will be used. Because the participants engaged in free recall, whereby they were expected to remember as much as possible about the reading, this likely assisted them later when asked to write down everything they remembered. The other hypothesis is that the act of retrieving the information assists with elaborative processes that create a semantic network that is more readily accessed. Remembering reinforces the organizational structure of the memory.

Regardless of the specific phenomenon underlying test-enhanced learning (and likely both of the aforementioned contribute in some way), the benefits of testing are manifold. Importantly, this particular technique has been evidence-validated in "simulated" (Butler & Roediger, 2007) as well as real (middle school science; McDaniel, Agarwal, Huelser, McDermott, & Roediger, 2011) classroom settings.

Though the transfer-appropriate processing encoding hypothesis would suggest that having a review or recall session soon after first reading the material would be the most helpful for later memory (because of the proximity to initial encoding), in fact, a review quiz (closer to when a unit exam was to be administered than when the lesson was presented) or a post-lesson quiz were found to be of equal benefit (McDaniel, Agarwal, Huelser, McDermott, & Roediger, 2011).

Though multiple-choice quizzes are effective in triggering test-enhanced learning (McDaniel, Agarwal, Huelser, McDermott, & Roediger,

2011), free recall assessments probably work best and whenever possible quizzes should utilize this format.

This phenomenon is so robust that even material that isn't directly assessed will be enhanced by test-enhanced learning. This phenomenon, which is called retrieval-induced facilitation (Chan, McDermott, & Roediger, 2006), means that even if 12 ideas (out of 24) were present on a quiz or test, the act of quizzing would also enhance memory for the other, non-tested 12.

Remember that in lab and classroom demonstrations of test-enhanced learning, participants in the "test" groups weren't allowed to study per se before the test. The testing *was* the studying. Put differently, retrieval-induced facilitation doesn't occur because participants study more in anticipation of the test. Rather, it is the test itself that causes the enhancement, even for non-tested material. This likely occurs because the information that is tested activates the full semantic network for all of the ideas that are associated with it, thus the entire engram likely undergoes plasticity-dependent strengthening.

Both the educational ramifications and the recommendations for implementation are fairly self-evident here. Whenever possible, introduce opportunities for students to retrieve information. Whether as a test review or a post-lesson wrap-up, the sheer act of having to recall facts and concepts that have been learned will actually enhance the storage for those as well as all associated (i.e., retrieval-induced facilitation) ideas. Though free recall is preferred, if time limitations (and we all know that time is a precious classroom commodity) make the choice between a multiple-choice quiz or no quiz at all, go with the multiple-choice quiz—evidence demonstrates that it will help.

RETRIEVAL AS RE-ENCODING

Try to recall what word was used in the last chapter to demonstrate priming. If you can't remember it yet, I'll give you a hint, it began with the three letters CON-. As you were just now retrieving the word from your long-term memory store, you were forming an episodic memory of yourself in the present trying to remember your prior memory (Tulving et al., 1994). This means that whenever anyone retrieves semantic information from long-term memory, they are also simultaneously encoding a new memory, and that memory is episodic in nature. The same phenomenon holds true when one tries to remember an episodic memory. Namely, that a new episodic memory is formed through the act of recalling the episodic memory!

The ramification of the *re-encoding* of information through retrieval (sometimes called *reconsolidation* by cognitive researchers) is that memories can be, and, indeed, are modified when we remember them. This is nicely illustrated in the next study. Researchers solicited participants who had been to a Disney theme park at some point in their life (Braun, Ellis, & Loftus, 2002). These participants were brought into the laboratory and were asked to read a fictional advertisement for Disneyland (this study took place in California) that asked the reader to remember a time when s/he went racing through Disneyland or Disney World as a child.

The ad was written to tap into several different senses, including sight, hearing, olfaction (our sense of smell), and even the feeling of having one's heart racing. At the end of the ad, there was either a small description of the excitement felt when meeting Bugs Bunny at the park or a description of something unrelated to the cartoon rabbit.

Two weeks after the participants read the advertisement, they were asked to return to the laboratory where they were asked to remember back to a time when they personally had visited a Disney park. It is important to note here that when brought back, there was no mention of the advertisement that had been read. Shockingly, the researchers found that over 25 percent of the participants who had read the modified advertisement actually remembered personally seeing or meeting Bugs Bunny as a child. Given the fact that Bugs Bunny belongs to the pantheon of Warner Brothers cartoon characters and not those of the Walt Disney Corporation, it is not surprising that none of the control group (i.e., those who read an ad with no mention of Bugs Bunny) remembered any such sighting or meeting. What's more, the percentage of participants who remembered this unlikely, if not impossible, meeting was increased for a subset of the experimental group who read the modified advertisement when a cardboard cut-out of Bugs Bunny was also present in the room (at the time of encoding).

We can make sense of findings such as these if we consider our memories as depositories of information. Indeed, I find it useful to visualize our memories as the vast government warehouse from the end of *Raiders of the Lost Ark* (which was revisited in *Indiana Jones and the Kingdom of the Crystal Skull*). That warehouse was full of crates and boxes stacked floor-to-ceiling. Within our own mental warehouse, one can envision file cabinets stacked similarly and within those cabinets reside all of our memories.

When we recall something, like our own trip to Disneyland, we must trek through the warehouse, find the correct file cabinet and retrieve the proper file folder. Within this folder are all of the separate sensory components—the images, sounds, and so forth (the papers within the file folder)—associated with that memory. When we recognize something, like Bugs Bunny, we do so because we have a stored memory—a file folder—for it.

When we have two or more memory folders open, such as one for our trip to Disney and one relating to Bugs Bunny, there is the possibility that files from one folder could be mistakenly placed in another folder. Indeed, as Loftus and colleagues showed, this in fact does happen.

Because of the size of our mental warehouse, and the fact that we need to put away folders no longer being used to make room for new folders (remember, working memory has limited capacity), the misfiling of information, the cross-contamination of memories, can take place without our ever realizing it. Then, the next time we go back to that memory file folder and open it, we peruse its contents and just assume that they are all correct. This is how we *misremember* seeing or meeting Bugs Bunny at Disneyland.

Results such as these are shocking. It is unsettling to think that people's memories can be manipulated so easily; yet, this is in fact the case. Though only one study was just referenced, there are literally dozens that demonstrate similar results using different stimuli, situations, and experiences. Indeed, the work of Dr. Loftus and like-minded researchers who study false memories has broad ramifications for law enforcement officials, therapists, and attorneys. But what about teachers?

Though educators need not be too worried about inadvertently changing existing vacation memories for students, they should be aware of how easy it is to influence retrieval, in particular for semantic memory, through similar processes. In one well-established experimental paradigm, participants are shown a number of words from a list and then after a period of time, meant to distract them from consciously rehearsing the words in their minds using the phonoarticulatory loop, their recall of the words is assessed. Let's try it with the next list of words.

Read each one and when you're all done cover the page and count backward from 30 before writing down all of the words you can recall:

| PANE | DOOR | SASH | GLASS | SILL | OPEN |
| LEDGE | CURTAIN | BREEZE | SHUTTER | VIEW | SHADE |

Now that you've written down all of your words, compare your list against the one just given and see if you've written down any words that weren't in the list. A word likely to appear in your list though it wasn't presented here is "WINDOW" (Roediger & McDermott, 1995). Because all of these words are semantically related to the concept of WINDOW, the network for that word becomes activated along with all of the words actually seen.

It may even be strongly activated as all of the words work together to activate it. When we then go to retrieve the words we've seen, it is those mental nodes within our semantic networks that were the most strongly activated that will be the ones most likely to be remembered, regardless if they were actually seen or not.

Semantic relatedness is one reason why we most often remember the *gist* of what we have experienced or learned, while recollection of details often eludes us. To prompt for details, we need to be sure that our prompts are specific and easily understood. In a history class, rather than asking "What happened at Appomattox Court House?," which could yield any number of somewhat correct answers, including "a battle," "a surrender," and so on, one would request that the student "describe the events of April 9, 1865, that led to the eventual surrender of the Confederate Army later that day at Appomattox Court House."

Not only does the semantic relatedness of words affect what we remember but the manner in which we ask makes a difference as well. It has been shown that eyewitness estimates of the speed with which two cars were traveling increase by 25 percent when eyewitnesses are asked "About how fast were the cars going when they *smashed* into each other" rather than "About how fast were the cars going when they *contacted* each other" (Loftus & Palmer, 1974).

Thus *how* we phrase a question matters as much as what we ask. This has repercussions for pedagogy as well as classroom management. When investigating a fight or some allegation of misconduct, the teacher must be careful to not ask questions that lead the student to remember the conclusion suggested by the question. Thus asking students to "comment on the choices made by the traitorous Brutus in yesterday's reading" will likely result in more accurate answers than "comment on the choices made by Brutus in yesterday's reading."

If one is interested, however, not in more correct answers but rather whether students can correctly identify and recognize Brutus as disloyal and then provide context for why his choices were so harmful, then the latter phrasing would be better.

Probing words should be used judiciously and purposefully. Furthermore, there should be consideration given for recall of gist material. If specific details are required from a student, then a recognition test, such as occurs with multiple-choice format assessments, may be ideal. Though multiple choice tests have been lamented as not allowing for expression of the type of higher-order critical reasoning skills that are often desired by teachers, when thoughtfully written, with careful consideration of the role played by distracter items (i.e., those options that are not correct), they can be effective ways to assess for knowledge (and even application) of phenomena (Little, Bjork, Bjork, & Angello, 2012). Given the cognitive factors underlying retrieval, it is recommended that formative assessments incorporate items that assess recognition (e.g., multiple choice) as well as recall (e.g., essay questions).

REVISITING EMOTIONAL AROUSAL AND MEMORY

Much was said in the last chapter about the enhancing effects of emotion on memory. The fact that research has shown time and time again that physiological activation (i.e., arousal) is beneficial for memory may have given some of you pause. After all, in your own experiences, either as an educator or as a student, you may have experienced circumstances whereby it seemed as though your emotions actually *impaired* memory. And indeed, your recollection of the roadblock that emotion placed in your own path to remembering is consistent with what research has shown. This is because, as we will soon see, the effects of emotion upon *encoding* are different from those upon *retrieval*.

Next, we must also differentiate between short-term or acute fluctuations in arousal and the more long-lived conditions of stress and anxiety. You may recall from chapter 5 that the amygdala is responsible for our emotional reactions to stimuli. After appraising the situation, the amygdala acts upon the hippocampus as well as other structures, including the hypothalamus. The amygdalar activation of the hypothalamus activates what is known as the "HPA" axis, whereby the "H" stands for hypothalamus, the "P" for pituitary, and the "A" for adrenal glands.

As briefly mentioned earlier, the hypothalamus activates the pituitary gland (via release of corticotrophin-releasing hormone; CRH), which then releases adrenocorticotrophic hormone (ACTH), which signals the adrenal glands to release both adrenaline and cortisol (Herman & Cullinan, 1997).

The adrenaline that is released into the bloodstream cannot act directly upon the brain (due to what is called the "blood-brain barrier") but must be converted into brain-accessible compounds, such as epinephrine, that then maintain activation of the amygdala in a feed-forward loop of amygdala activation leading to adrenaline release, which then maintains amygdala activation, leading to more adrenaline release, and so forth.

The action of adrenaline upon the hippocampus, which as we know is critical for conversion of short-term memories into those lasting a lifetime, through the amygdala is indirect. Whether or not a threat is perceived will determine the extent to which the amygdala and downstream structures within the HPA axis stay in "alert" mode or not.

Unlike adrenaline, cortisol can pass through the blood-brain barrier and act directly upon the hippocampus and other brain structures that are critical for memory storage. Receptors for cortisol are found throughout the brain, including the same areas of the frontal cortex that are necessary for memory retrieval. The locations of these receptors are critical because cortisol, in the short-term, has a deactivating or inhibiting effect upon neurons (e.g., Lyons, Lopez, Yang, & Schatzberg, 2000).

In the long-term, the effects of cortisol on the brain are more insidious. Long-term, chronic exposure to cortisol results in death of brain cells, either through dose-dependent toxicity (Leverenz et al., 1999) or apoptosis, which is a bizarre phenomenon whereby cells engage a set of mechanisms to kill themselves, in other words, cellular suicide (Fuchs & Steller, 2011).

In addition, within the hippocampus, cortisol levels actually decrease the number of newly born cells that can be successfully integrated into existing cellular populations (Gould & Tanapat, 1999). The hippocampus is one of only a few sites within the *adult* brain where new neurons continue to be born throughout our lives (Eriksson et al., 1998), and the survival of these cells is involved in the normal functioning of memory processes (Deng, Aimone, & Gage, 2010).

There are many ways that stress and prolonged arousal can have negative effects upon the brain. But why are these effects largely restricted to impairing retrieval processes and not encoding? Though for most Americans, September 11, 2001, was an incredibly stressful, fear- and anxiety-filled day, each of us has a vivid memory of where we were and what we were doing when we first found out that airplanes had collided with the towers of the World Trade Center, the Pentagon, and crashed in a field in Pennsylvania. It turns out that though our brains evolved to store information that we are presented with during times of heightened emotional arousal, the same cannot be said about later *retrieving* information when under duress.

Why is stress and anxiety so debilitating to test performance? Though we have already covered the physiological reasons, in particular the nasty effects of cortisol upon the brain, there may be an evolutionary explanation as well. To explore this reason, we first need to rewind the clock to the time when our early ancestors were first emerging as a species distinct from other primates (i.e., several *million* years ago; Hasegawa, Kishino, & Yano, 1985).

At that point in our survival, there were a number of large predators, as well as other hominids (i.e., human-like primates, such as Neanderthals, who, though related to us, are not our direct ancestors; Currat & Excoffier, 2004), who were real and actual threats. Of our ancestors, those who were most likely to survive were those who were not only able to identify the threats successfully the first time (thus escaping) but also remember salient features about those threats. Though life spans at that point in time were probably more accurately measured in years than decades, all that needed to happen was for an individual to survive long enough to pass his/her genes to offspring.

Natural selection tells us that those species that are able to survive will pass on the genes and traits that facilitated their survival in the first place (Darwin, 1859). Thus those primitive individuals who had the most well-developed and sensitive amygdalas were likely the ones to survive long enough to create descendants who also had well-developed and sensitive amygdalas.

Now let's fast forward the clock to present-day life. Here we are, the byproduct of all of those primitive struggles for survival, living our present-day existences in civilization. We are here as a byproduct of our ancestors having sensitive threat detectors (amygdala), which we in turn inherited. However, those threat detectors that were so well-adapted to primitive times, able to identify and remember all of the threats to existence that occurred on a daily, if not hourly, basis, may not be so well-suited to modern-day living. Most of us are lucky that we don't have all of the base, physical struggles for survival that our primitive ancestors did. However, this fact has been lost on our amygdala.

Because we are hardwired to detect threats (and remember, if our ancestors weren't, we probably wouldn't be here), our amygdala must now identify threats that don't actually directly affect our survival. For this reason, we overreact in emotional settings. We suffer from mass road rage and we panic over quizzes and exams that in no way directly affect any of our basic needs as humans (i.e., Maslow, 1943).

Thus, reducing the anxiety and stress is paramount to successful academic performance. Unfortunately, this fact has been lost on the legislators who have attached incredible significance to examinations as a result of the No Child Left Behind act of 2002. Particularly, because we know that the stress that is experienced by classroom teachers may trickle down to students and impair their learning (Flink, Boggiano, & Barrett, 1990).

Stress does not impact all individuals the same. One psychological factor that mediates the effects of stress upon retrieval is extroversion/introversion. Though the popular usage of the term "introversion" is used to imply someone who is shy and socially awkward, this is actually not an accurate description of this particular personality component.

Every person has an optimal level of arousal. The well-documented relationship between arousal and cognitive performance (on tasks relevant to classroom settings) is an inverted U-shape (Yerkes & Dodson, 1908), with arousal on the x-axis and performance on the y-axis. For each individual, there is a level of arousal that corresponds to peak performance: the optimal level for that person. It turns out that human beings seek out this optimal level because it provides a balance between too little arousal (e.g., bored) and too much (e.g., over-anxious).

Each person's optimal level is determined by his/her level of extroversion. All things being equal, extroverts have lower levels of baseline arousal than do introverts. Thus extroverts seek out external stimuli that will increase their levels of arousal. These stimuli can take any number of different forms, including auditory, visual, or even social. My wife, a brilliant woman, is an extrovert. I remember when she was working on her dissertation in graduate school or writing an article, she would actually need to have the television on in the background. The television provided her with enough of an arousal "kick" that her level of arousal became optimal.

I, on the other hand, am more of an introvert. This means that my body supplies a high enough level of arousal that I don't need external stimuli. In fact, because I am already operating close to my optimal level of arousal, external stimuli can have a debilitating effect. Being already at the top of the inverted "U" means that any increases in arousal will move me toward decreasing levels of performance. In fact, as I work on this section of the book I am doing so at 5:42 in the morning. Why? Because my house is quiet and I can efficiently and effectively (at least I like to think so) write. External stimuli, such as the television, radio, or children, would prove too disruptive (i.e., increase my level of arousal) to this process.

Studies have shown that increasing the level of pressure surrounding an examination affects introverts more than extroverts (Alpert & Haber, 1960). Cognitive differences are likely due to neurological differences. In support, the brains of extroverts and introverts look different when imaged while performing cognitive tasks. Extroverts have less connectivity in some brain regions (Wright et al., 2006) than introverts, which may be the neurological basis for this personality trait.

The greater connectivity in the brains of introverts may be why they are normally operating closer to peak efficiency. Because of these neurological differences, extroverts must seek out arousal from other sources, such as social settings. Thus it isn't that extroverts are more gregarious and socially comfortable, it is that they are in effect "stimulus vampires," sustaining themselves on the arousal of others.

Taken together, many of the strategies of this chapter and the one before it can be used in concert to maximize learning and facilitate successful retrieval of learned material. The testing effect, covered in this chapter, is particularly useful and robust, having a wealth of evidence, both in the laboratory and classrooms, to support its integration into any lesson plan.

POINTS TO REMEMBER:

- Many of the same brain structures used to learn material are also used when we remember.
- The hippocampus binds together various elements (cues) of a memory. If the memory is stored successfully, then any of the individual cues should be sufficient to retrieve the memory.
- Retrieval is facilitated by the semantic organization of information within the brain.
- People store information similarly—both in terms of where the engram is stored in the brain and how the information is organized.
- The context associated with the physical space where learning takes place holds many cues for memory retrieval.
- Testing enhances memory, even for items not present in the exam. Test-enhanced learning has been repeatedly shown to be more ef-

fective than repeatedly studying material, even when no feedback was given on test performance.
- A memory can be modified every time it is remembered. Episodic memories are particularly susceptible to memory distortions.
- The way that a question is asked can influence how answers are recalled.
- Though arousal enhances learning, it impairs retrieval. There are some differences in the effects of arousal on learning for extroverts and introverts.
- Extroverts require more stimulation from the external environment so that they may reach their optimal level of arousal. Introverts are closer to their optimal level and thus require less.

REFERENCES

Alpert, R., & Haber, R. N. (1960). Anxiety in academic achievement situations. *The Journal of Abnormal and Social Psychology, 61*(2), 207–215.
Braun, K. A., Ellis, R., & Loftus, E. F. (2002). Make my memory: How advertising can change our memories of the past. *Psychology and Marketing, 19*(1), 1–23.
Brown, R., & McNeill, D. (1966). The "tip of the tongue" phenomenon. *Journal of Verbal Learning and Verbal Behavior, 5*(4), 325–337.
Butler, A. C., & Roediger, H. L. (2007). Testing improves long-term retention in a simulated classroom setting. *European Journal of Cognitive Psychology, 19*, 514–527.
Chan, C. K., McDermott, K. B., & Roediger, H. L. (2006). Retrieval induced facilitation: Initially nontested material can benefit from prior testing. *Journal of Experimental Psychology: General, 135*, 533–571.
Corkin, S. (2002). What's new with the amnesic patient HM? *Nature Reviews Neuroscience, 3*(2), 153–160.
Currat, M., & Excoffier, L. (2004). Modern humans did not admix with Neanderthals during their range expansion into Europe. *PLoS biology, 2*(12), e421.
Damasio, H., Grabowski, T. J., Tranel, D., Hichwa, R. D., & Damasio, A. R. (1996). A 1 neural basis for lexical retrieval. *Nature, 380*(6574), 499–505.
Darwin, C. (1936). *The origin of species by means of natural selection.* New York: Modern Library. (Original work published 1859).
Deng, W., Aimone, J. B., & Gage, F. H. (2010). New neurons and new memories: How does adult hippocampal neurogenesis affect learning and memory? *Nature Reviews Neuroscience, 11*(5), 339–350.
Duncan, C. P. (1949). The retroactive effect of electroshock on learning. *Journal of Comparative and Physiological Psychology, 42*(1), 32–44.
Ebbinghaus, H. (1885). *Memory: A contribution to experimental psychology.* New York: Teachers College, Columbia University.
Eriksson, P. S., Perfilieva, E., Björk-Eriksson, T., Alborn, A. M., Nordborg, C., Peterson, D. A., & Gage, F. H. (1998). Neurogenesis in the adult human hippocampus. *Nature medicine, 4*(11), 1313–1317.
Flink, C., Boggiano, A. K., & Barrett, M. (1990). Controlling teaching strategies: Undermining children's self-determination and performance. *Journal of Personality and Social Psychology, 59*(5), 916–924.
Fuchs, Y., & Steller, H. (2011). Programmed cell death in animal development and disease. *Cell, 147*(4), 742–758.
Gould, E., & Tanapat, P. (1999). Stress and hippocampal neurogenesis. *Biological psychiatry, 46*(11), 1472–1479.

Hasegawa, M., Kishino, H., & Yano, T. A. (1985). Dating of the human-ape splitting by a molecular clock of mitochondrial DNA. *Journal of Molecular Evolution*, 22(2), 160–174.

Herman, J. P., & Cullinan, W. E. (1997). Neurocircuitry of stress: Central control of the hypothalamo–pituitary–adrenocortical axis. *Trends in Neurosciences*, 20(2), 78–84.

Leverenz, J. B., Wilkinson, C. W., Wamble, M., Corbin, S., Grabber, J. E., Raskind, M. A., & Peskind, E. R. (1999). Effect of chronic high-dose exogenous cortisol on hippocampal neuronal number in aged nonhuman primates. *The Journal of Neuroscience*, 19(6), 2356–2361.

Little, J. L., Bjork, E. L., Bjork, R. A., & Angello, G. (2012). Multiple-choice tests exonerated, at least of some charges fostering test-induced learning and avoiding test-induced forgetting. *Psychological Science*, 23(11), 1337–1344.

Loftus, E.F., & Palmer, J.C. (1974). Reconstruction of auto-mobile destruction: An example of the interaction between language and memory. *Journal of Verbal Learning and Verbal Behaviour*, 13, 585 -589.

Lyons, D. M., Lopez, J. M., Yang, C., & Schatzberg, A. F. (2000). Stress-level cortisol treatment impairs inhibitory control of behavior in monkeys. *The Journal of Neuroscience*, 20(20), 7816–7821.

Maslow, A. H. (1943). A theory of human motivation. *Psychological Review*, 50, 370–396.

McDaniel, M. A., Agarwal, P. K., Huelser, B. J., McDermott, K. B., & Roediger, H. L. (2011). Test-enhanced learning in a middle school science classroom: The effects of quiz frequency and placement. *Journal of Educational Psychology*, 103, 399–414.

McDaniel, M. A., & Masson, M. E. J. (1985). Altering memory representations through retrieval. *Journal of Experimental Psychology: Learning, Memory, and Cognition*, 11, 371–385.

Morris, C. D., Bransford, J. D., & Franks, J. J. (1977). Levels of processing versus transfer-appropriate processing. *Journal of Verbal Learning and Verbal Behavior*, 16, 519–533.

Rekart, J.L., & Routtenberg, A. (2008). Post-translational brain protein modification as substrate for memories that last a lifetime. *BioTech International*, 20(5), 6-8.

Roediger, H. L., & McDermott, K. B. (1995). Creating false memories: Remembering words not presented in lists. *Journal of Experimental Psychology: Learning, Memory, and Cognition*, 21(4), 803.

Roediger, H. L., & Karpicke, J. D. (2006). Test-enhanced learning: Taking memory tests improves long-term retention. *Psychological Science*, 17, 249–255.

Rosch, E., & Mervis, C. B. (1975). Family resemblances: Studies in the internal structure of categories. *Cognitive Psychology*, 7(4), 573–605.

Smith, S. M., Glenberg, A., & Bjork, R. A. (1978). Environmental context and human memory. *Memory & Cognition*, 6(4), 342–353.

Squire, L. R., Slater, P. C., & Chace, P. M. (1975). Retrograde amnesia: Temporal gradient in very long-term memory following electroconvulsive therapy. *Science*, 187(4171), 77–79.

Tulving, E., Kapur, S., Craik, F. M., Moscovitch, M., & Houle, S. (1994). Hemispheric encoding/retrieval asymmetry in episodic memory: Positron emission tomography findings. *Proceedings of the National Academy of Sciences, U.S.A.*, 91, 2016–2020.

Van Der Wege, M., & Barry, L. A. (2008). Potential perils of changing environmental context on examination scores. *College Teaching*, 56(3), 173–176.

Wright, C. I., Williams, D., Feczko, E., Barrett, L. F., Dickerson, B. C., Schwartz, C. E., & Wedig, M. M. (2006). Neuroanatomical correlates of extraversion and neuroticism. *Cerebral Cortex*, 16(12), 1809–1819.

Yerkes R. M., & Dodson J. D. (1908). The relation of strength of stimulus to rapidity of habit-formation. *Journal of Comparative Neurology and Psychology*, 18, 459–482.

SEVEN
Language

Take a moment and try to recall your earliest memory. Yes, this chapter covers language, but it never hurts to review (or quiz oneself on) what we've already covered. Chances are good that your memory has some emotion associated with it. For example, it may revolve around an accident or someone close to you leaving. Alternatively, it may be a birthday (perhaps your third or fourth) or when a newly born sibling was first introduced to you. Though I cannot presume to know specifically *what* it is that you recalled when asked to retrieve your earliest memory, I can state unequivocally that the memory you believe to be your *oldest* in fact is not.

You are probably thinking that this is a fairly bold statement. Let's review how it is that I know, without a shadow of a doubt, that what you think of as your first memory is in fact one that occurred much later in your life. First, remember that memory consists of both declarative and non-declarative forms of information. Thus there are skills and associations that we have, say the attachment for a parent, that extend back to some of our earliest moments in infancy.

Though this is all true, I wasn't trying to be that tricky. After all, for the past few chapters we have only been discussing declarative memories when we talk about "long-term" memories. So, even then, chances are excellent that you failed to actually identify what your earliest memories are. Why? Because they were semantic. In fact, this is why this question appears in this chapter, because many of our earliest semantic memories, those that we still use and carry with us to this day, are those related to our understanding and use of language.

Remember, our memories represent stored information that is portable. Words like "Mama," "Dada," "up," and "more" had to be learned. You know that the sounds \mä-mə\ refer to the woman who gave birth to you because the association between the sounds and an individual person was first encoded when your age was more appropriately measured in months than in years. Every time you know what those sounds mean, to whom they refer, and all of the other characteristics associated with your mother or mothers in general, you are retrieving one of your, if not *the*, oldest memories.

In this chapter, we will explore the cognitive basis of communication and discuss how words and different forms of language can inform and enhance pedagogy. By examining the relationship of language with some of the foundational processes of cognition (i.e., attention and memory), we will gain a fuller understanding of how it, in turn, influences reasoning and decision making.

LANGUAGE AND THE BRAIN

In April of 1861 the French physician Paul Broca first came into contact with a patient who could hear and understand language without issue but could not produce any intelligible sound other the word "tan," which he would repeat in response to all inquiries (Broca, 1861). In addition to being an epileptic, this patient had a number of other issues and subsequently died within a week of first meeting Broca. Upon autopsy, Broca made note of a "softening" of tissue that was largely restricted to the upper frontal lobe, around what were described as the "2nd and 3rd convolutions" (Broca, 1861).

Thirteen years later, Carl Wernicke published an account of several patients who had damage to the first convolution of the left temporal lobe, which left speech intact but severely impacted those patients' ability to comprehend spoken language. These two findings, and the eponymous anatomical loci, mark the beginning of our understanding of the neurological basis of language.

Over a century later, our understanding of how the brain facilitates communication has expanded upon the classic work of Broca and Wernicke. For example, though our understanding of the importance of those two areas and the roles that they play in speech production and comprehension, respectively, have not changed, we now know that there is even more cortical tissue devoted to our ability to transmit and understand information than was previously thought.

Connecting the two production and comprehension areas of the brain is a large bundle of axons called the *arcuate fasciculus* (Friederici, 2009). The arcuate facilitates bidirectional communication between Broca's and Wernicke's areas; speaking facilitates comprehension and vice versa. In addition, the arcuate fasciculus also integrates information from what is considered a higher-order language processing center, the inferior parietal lobule, an area often referred to as "Geschwind's territory" after the neuroanatomist whose early work predicted the importance of this region (Geschwind, 1965).

An examination of the amount of brain tissue necessary for a particular behavior or mental process can lead one to infer several things about the process. It may be that so much tissue is required, assuming that nature and evolution prefer economy, only because the process is complicated and complex. Alternatively, though not necessarily mutually exclusive, it may be that the region is of incredible importance to the animal's survival.

When one examines the distribution of cortical surface area across three cerebral lobes that are devoted to language, it is easy to see how language is both a challenging endeavor and one that was critical to our survival and success as a species.

Think about everyday usage of language that we take for granted. "The girl was hot" can have any number of different meanings. It may indicate that the girl feels as though the thermostat is too high. Or perhaps the girl has a fever. Alternatively, the speaker could be trying to convey that s/he finds the girl to be sexually attractive. The fact that the same word, "hot," can have three very different meanings (ranging from one's perceptions of the physical temperature to a sign of illness to an external appraisal of one's attractiveness), and yet we can easily and quickly decipher meaning from the context, knowledge of the speaker, and so forth speaks to the ease with which neural systems handle a complicated process.

HANDS DOWN, GESTURES ARE IMPORTANT FOR COGNITION

Though we will certainly address oral speech, it bears mentioning that there are other ways that humans communicate with one another. Body language is used by humans and nonhuman animals to convey important information ranging from the presence of a predator to where food is located (de Gelder, 2006). Brain regions involved in emotional body language exist outside those normally used for speech-related communication, including the amygdala, ventromedial prefrontal cortex, and the premotor cortex (de Gelder, 2006).

One form of nonverbal communication of particular importance to education is the use of hand gestures. Think about a time when you knew the answer to a question but couldn't quite put your finger (literally) on what that answer was. In that situation, you may have made motions with your hands, perhaps without even realizing you were doing so, as you tried to recall the information that was in your mind. Indeed, we now know that, in fact, those gestures may have signaled your brain's attempts to access verbal information that may have been related to the answer. Put differently, they were an outward signal of your attempt to retrieve communicable information.

Interestingly, gesturing may, in fact, facilitate retrieval of verbal information from the brain during the normal course of conversation. Before discussing such findings, we must first differentiate between two types of gestures that people use when speaking. The first, *motor gestures*, are repetitive and brief movements that don't appear to relate to anything that is being spoken (Hadar, 1989). The second, which are of interest here, are *lexical gestures*, which last longer than motor gestures and actually seem to convey information that is related to what is being spoken (Hadar, 1989).

When participants were asked to describe a scene that they had observed, there was an increment in the amount of time required to speak if they were prevented from gesturing while speaking. In addition, when trying to describe what are referred to as "spatial" components of the scene, meaning those components that have to do with three-dimensional space and the relation of objects to one another within it (in this study, spatial aspects were identified by prepositions used, such as "above," "between," etc.), non-gesturers made more pauses and had more dysfluencies than gesturers (Rauscher, Krauss, & Chen, 1996).

Gestures are necessary for cognition and should be allowed during normal speech interactions. Indeed, when teachers are allowed to gesture, preschool students have been shown to learn concepts better (Valenzeno, Alibali, & Klatzky, 2003). You may be asking yourself, what kind of gesturing was used, particularly as we have already differentiated between gestures that activate and involve higher-order cognitive centers (i.e., lexical gestures) and those that do not (i.e., motor gestures). In the study just cited, the lesson involved the concepts of symmetry and the gestures consisted of nothing more than pointing and tracing examples in the air with one's fingers. Thus the gestures that are being used are (1) natural and (2) germane.

But can gestures, on their own, actually enhance learning if introduced where they aren't naturally used? Broaders and colleagues (2007) examined this question with third and fourth graders learning math. Students were told either to gesture when learning a novel concept while solving problems at a blackboard or to avoid gesturing when learning the concept. The researchers found that by having the students actively use gestures to solve the problems, many of them added new strategies for problem solving to their repertoire. These strategies were then directly related to enhanced performance on a follow-up post-test, with gesturing students outperforming non-gesturing students by close to 40 percent.

Given the work of Valenzeno et al. (2003), reviewed previously, one could argue that the striking difference between the gesturing and non-gesturing group could be due more to an impairment of the ability of the non-gesturing group to perform rather than an enhancement of the group explicitly directed to use their hands. To account for this, Broaders et al. actually examined the number of novel problem-solving strategies that were facilitated by gesturing between students told to gesture, asked not to gesture, and students given no explicit instructions (a control group).

First, there was no significant difference in the number of gestures produced by students told to gesture and those who were allowed to do so spontaneously (the control group). There was, however, a four-fold difference in the number of novel strategies between students in the control condition and the gesture conditions, but no significant difference was reported between the spontaneous and non-gesturing groups. Because it was the gesture-induced novel strategies that were found to mediate the enhanced performance and learning on the post-test, it is likely that encouraging students to use their hands facilitated learning.

The use of gestures also seems to produce learning that is long-lasting. Directly after instruction, there is no difference in the degree of understanding between students taught mathematical equivalencies using speech and gestures and those taught using only speech instructions. However, when learning was examined four-weeks later, students who learned using gestures retained 85 percent of the knowledge that they exhibited immediately after instruction (based on a post-test) compared with only 33 percent retention for students taught without gestures (Cook, Mitchell, & Goldin-Meadow, 2008).

Similar long-term gains were seen when young children were taught about the preposition "under." Those children who were instructed by teachers using hand gestures had longer-lasting and more fully developed understanding of the concept of "under" than those children who were taught using images (thus both involved visual demonstrations; McGregor, Rohlfing, Bean, & Marschner, 2009).

The effects of gestures upon learning appear to be efficacious across the lifespan. Long-term retention and understanding of a second language was shown to be enhanced when adults were taught by instructors who used speech-consistent gestures in their instruction (Kelly, McDevitt, & Esch, 2009).

So what is it about hand gestures that makes them such an important tool for learning? Preliminary neurological data suggest that learning that involves hand gestures activates some association areas in the parietal cortex (Kelly, McDevitt, & Esch, 2009) that aren't observed when only verbal instructions are received. The recruitment of a greater number of areas during learning likely leads to a more diffuse memory network, which has been theorized as contributing to longer-lasting memories (Rekart & Routtenberg, 2008).

It is known that activation of the motor cortex accompanies the use of gestures when learning and that this activation is probably linked to the enhancing effects of manual movements upon learning (Macedonia & Knosche, 2011). However, even when students don't personally use gestures when learning new concepts, if they view someone else making gestures, the observation of those gestures should be sufficient to activate the motor neuron system, which is, in fact, what has been demonstrated (Montgomery, Isenberg, & Haxby, 2007).

Though the motor neuron system will be activated with the visualization of any gesture, when those manual movements actually are congruent with the concepts being taught (i.e., lexical gestures), then there will be a reinforcement of learning through the creation of a wider and more diffuse neural network.

It should be noted that the gesturing and learning studies discussed here, like almost all of the studies cited in this book, did not *a priori* divide students into any groups based on learning styles. This is an important distinction because the findings that have been discussed relate to how people *in general* communicate and learn. These findings are not representative of, related to, nor are they evidence for a kinesthetic learning style. They are rather evidence for the role that kinesthetics play in learning.

The use of gestures in instruction represents a simple and, perhaps more importantly, free instructional method that is both evidence based and evidence validated. It is worthwhile for instructors to look at their own practice and actively consider how and when to implement gestures into their teaching. Teachers should not feel as though a great deal of research must go into which gestures to use as the movements that are introduced can be quite simple.

For example, when learning about mathematical equivalencies such as:

$$4 + 5 + 3 = 2 + 6 + \underline{}$$

the teacher merely swept her left hand under the numbers to the left of the equal sign and then her right hand under the numbers (and the blank) to the right of the equal sign. When reading the problem, students were then instructed to do the same (Cook, Mitchell, & Goldin-Meadow, 2008).

When considering which gestures to use, teachers should think about whether the movements would be made naturally by someone trying to understand the problem. What should be avoided is crafting a whole new language or set of signs that will only serve to tax working memory and thus would likely impair learning.

AVOID STATEMENTS OF NEGATION AND THE PASSIVE VOICE

Some people may just be pessimists at heart. I, for example, will often state that something is "not a bad idea." This type of statement drives the people around me nuts, who wonder why I don't just say "it is a good idea" rather than negating a negative idea. They have a good point, for it turns out that most people actually think of the world in positive terms. Thus a negatively phrased statement, such as "It doesn't look like it will snow today," in actuality requires that two separate statements are processed cognitively for understanding.

The first is "It looks like snow today" and the second is "The preceding statement is false." Not surprisingly, because interpreting statements of negation involve twice as many interpretations (i.e., [1] the affirmatively phrased statement and [2] the realization that the first statement is false), it also requires more processing time (Wason, 1959). The increase in processing time is believed to be indicative of the increased cognitive load required to interpret statements that use words like "don't" and "not."

Because (most) humans translate statements of negation into affirmative statements and then address how the first statement is false, instructors should be mindful of their language. Whenever possible, use affirmatively phrased statements because otherwise statements of negation will (1) take cognitive resources away from the already-strapped working memory system and (2) take more time that could be spent keeping up with incoming information.

Evidence shows that the passive voice, the bane of high school English teachers everywhere, is harder to comprehend than the active voice. Not only does it take significantly longer to comprehend sentences that are written using the passive voice but people also make 10–15 percent more errors when describing the intent of passive sentences (Ferreira, 2003).

The cognitive bias here is similar to that discussed for statements of negation. Namely, passively constructed sentences must first be linguistically disassembled as active voices and then the subject and object of the verbs have to be determined. In contrast, in actively voiced sentences, the order of the words (i.e., subject-verb-object) is often used heuristically to decipher meaning, resulting in faster processing times. Just as with statements of negation, the increase in cognitive load leaves fewer resources available for other cognitive tasks, which may then impair working memory and attention.

Now, certainly the passive voice does have a place. You may have noticed that much of this text is actually written using the passive voice. As you may know, convention mandates that scientific writers use the passive voice. This is because in science, the phenomenon and not the researcher is of importance. For example, it is preferred that one writes that "Participants were asked to complete a survey," rather than "I asked participants to complete a survey," because the survey completion is what is critical. Regardless, conventional or not, it is important to note that comprehension of the passive voice requires more cognitive resources than the active.

LEARNING A LANGUAGE REQUIRES A PERSON

Most parents want to give their children a "leg up." In today's world, parents are anxious about job prospects for children who won't just be competing for work against the kid down the block but potentially the kids across the ocean. In the late 1990s and early 2000s, makers of "educational" DVDs (i.e., "baby media") targeted at small children exploited these anxieties to great economic success (Khermouch, 2004).

The idea was simple: sit your pre-linguistic child in front of the television, play the DVD, and, like magic, the child's vocabulary will expand beyond your wildest dreams. What's more, for approximately $14.99 parents had an on-call babysitter that was guilt free because, after all, the DVDs were "educational." Unfortunately, it is fairly evident now that the hype wasn't sufficient to ensure that the DVD equaled PhD.

Parents in large-scale studies have actually reported that, in fact, children exposed to baby media learned few, if any, of the words that were actually presented in the programs (Robb, Richert, & Wartella, 2009). Other surveys found a detrimental effect of baby media on infant lexical development. Specifically, those 8-to-16-month-olds who were exposed to baby media knew approximately seven words fewer for every hour of video watched per day than babies who were not exposed (Zimmerman, Christakis, & Meltzoff, 2007).

Though these aforementioned studies didn't say much about the promise of baby media in facilitating infant language development, they also didn't provide evidence that such videos actually impede normal language development. Because baby media was marketed as making "brainier babies," it stands to reason that those parents who were most concerned about their children may be the ones to use them. Thus it could be that the correlation between DVD viewing and poor language development was a reflection of the characteristics of the population of children and not the videos themselves.

To address this issue, a naturalistic experiment was conducted whereby children were exposed to a 39-minute commercial baby media DVD alone or with a parent, or were taught the same words found on the video with no TV exposure. The exposure groups had over ten hours of viewing time over a four-week period. Parent logs were used to make sure that viewing time or home instruction was all comparable. At the end of the four-week period, children's knowledge of the words taught by the videos/parents was assessed in their homes by researchers.

Consistent with the results of the correlational research, children exposed to infant educational videos learned fewer words than those instructed by parents. Whether the parent watched the video with the child or was merely in the room with him or her didn't make a difference; children who watched the video did not learn any more words than children who weren't exposed to the words at all (control condition; no television or parental instruction; De Loache et al., 2010).

The reason why baby media has no observable positive effect upon language development is likely similar to why gestural learning is so powerful: mirror neurons. Though definitive studies have not yet been published, evidence from both human and nonhuman primates suggest strongly that the mirror neuron system likely underlies our ability to both produce and comprehend communicative vocalizations, as well as gestures (Fogassi & Ferrari, 2012).

We know that even with intensive, daily exposure to video instruction in language, infants fail to maintain phonemic awareness (i.e., ability to differentiate between the sounds that are particular to a specific language) of the learned language, unlike infants who receive face-to-face instruction (Kuhl, Tsao, & Liu, 2003).

Whether such studies have any bearing on older children or adult learning remains to be determined. If similar results are seen with other subjects and age groups, as they have been with the acquisition of English in early childhood, it will seriously squelch the current fervor over "flipped classrooms," with the reliance on video delivery of lecture material (Sparks, 2011).

THE LANGUAGE OF MUSIC

Research is beginning to highlight the ways in which music and language are similar. From the use of the voice to speak or sing to commonalities in syntax, overlapping brain regions, and similar cognitive processes (Patel, 2003), these two fundamental human forms of communication play an important role in human development and happiness. Other similarities, unfortunately, may be found in the belief that exposure to pre-recorded media (i.e., CDs and DVDs) will somehow have enhancing effects upon cognition.

Before millions of DVDs of baby media were bought by parents in the late 90s, millions of CDs of sonatas by Mozart were purchased. Though as any adult who has viewed an infant DVD can attest, Mozart is a much better buy; any surges in consumer demand of his work weren't motivated by a renewed appreciation of his music. Rather, individuals were hoping to replicate the ill-interpreted findings (not by the authors but rather the media and the public) of short-term exposures to classical music leading to enhancements of spatial IQ (Rauscher, Shaw, & Ky, 1993).

The so-called "Mozart effect," which was named after the 1993 findings, was so popular that the then governor of Georgia, Zell Miller, even requested over $100,000 in funds to provide every new mother in the state with a CD of classical music to play for her baby (Sack, 1998). And why not? The findings suggested that increases in some aspects of spatial reasoning could be enjoyed by as little as ten minutes of exposure to classical music.

Unfortunately, this was another case of the evidence not supporting the claims that were made. Soon after the initial study was published, numerous independent attempts to replicate the effect failed (e.g., Steele, Bass, & Crook, 1999). Now, even though the authors themselves have put some distance between the article and their subsequent work (e.g., Rauscher & Hinton, 2006), the legend of the Mozart effect persists (Bangerter & Heath, 2004)—which is not to say that music doesn't serve a powerful role in our lives. We know that listening to music activates the brain's reward pathways, which involves a circuit of neurons that release and respond to dopamine, including the ventral tegmental area (VTA) and the nucleus accumbens (Menon & Levitin, 2005), both of which are also implicated in addiction. Thus there is a neurological reward associated with listening to music: pleasure.

It should be noted, however, that though listening to music does not seem to have a replicable or lasting effect on cognition, learning to play an instrument, in fact, may. This distinction has been raised by many scientists, including one of the original researchers responsible for the original "Mozart effect" (Rauscher & Hinton, 2006) and others (Črnčec, Wilson, & Prior, 2006). One of the original reports of music training–induced changes in cognition showed that six-year-old children who received either vocal or piano training for 36 weeks enjoyed an increase of 2.7 IQ points relative to children who received no training (Schellenberg, 2004). Though these results were significant, there were a few things to consider.

First, *all* of the children, whether receiving music instruction or not, actually showed increases of IQ. These increases were likely related to the fact that all of the children were entering formal schooling at the time of the study. Second, the actual difference in the increase between the musically trained children and those not receiving musical training was quite small. The standard deviation for IQ is 15 points, which means that on average any individual may be expected to differ from the average, which is 100, by about 15 points.

The difference that was observed is less than one-fifth of a standard deviation (0.18 to be exact), thus even with almost a year of formal music instruction, the impact was quite small. Finally, though the Schellenberg study was intriguing, there isn't much support for music-induced general enhancements in cognition.

Children who actively engage in musical instruction have been shown, in a number of studies, to have enhanced processing of auditory stimuli (for review see: Hannon & Trainor, 2007; Kraus & Chandresekaran, 2010). Active learning with musical instruments is consistent with modern neuroscientific theories of neural plasticity and Hebbian learning. Namely, those areas of the brain that are used the most, are developed. Though music does assist with mood regulation (not reviewed here) and is enjoyable, any effects it may have on cognition appear to affect the subsequent perception of sounds rather than globally enhance how well or efficiently one thinks in non-musical areas of their life.

LANGUAGE AND THOUGHT

Language is constantly evolving. As new words are added, like "texting," older words, like "typewriter" or "mimeograph," become obsolete. It is common for a high school student today to talk about her hundreds of *friends*, even though she may only spend quality face-to-face time with four or five people. Indeed, the evolution of the word *friend* from someone that is a confidant and trusted companion to someone who clicks a box on a computer screen speaks to the way in which even preexisting words take on new and different meanings.

Even though the same word may be used for a *traditional* friend and one gained through Facebook, the two words have different connotations in different contexts. Given the fact that words are what we use to not only communicate with others but also to think about our own inner lives, beliefs, and desires, one may wonder whether the actual words that we choose influence how we think.

In his classic papers on the relationship between language and thought, Benjamin Whorf often used examples of how different cultures used very different words. For example, though English has one word for "water," the Hopi language has two. On the other hand, in Hopi there is one word for everything that is not a bird that flies; English has many (Whorf, 1940). We will not talk here about language strictly *determining* thought, which may be closer to Whorf (and others') theories; we will discuss the more generally accepted theory that language *influences* how we think.

Just as Whorf did, modern researchers examine relationships between language and thought by examining different cultures. Though both native English speakers and Chinese speakers of Mandarin use "left" and "right" body-specific positions to think about time, Mandarin speakers also employ the vertical axis of directions to think about temporal relations (Boroditsky, Fuhrman, & McCormick, 2011).

English speakers often think of earlier events occurring to the left; in Mandarin earlier events may also be "up" and later events "down." Indeed, there are even some cultures that don't use "left" or "right" at all. The Pormpuraawans, an Aboriginal people from Australia, refer to objects using compass directions like "east" and "north" rather than "left" or "in front of you." Imagine going to someone's house and asking which drawer contained the silverware only to be told the northeast one. Because of these linguistic differences, how the Pormpuraawan think about and report time is markedly different from how English speakers do (Boroditsky & Gaby, 2010).

Linguistic differences between the Pormpuraawans and English speakers have further ramifications for thought. Though only 36 percent of English speakers could correctly identify the direction they were facing (within roughly 20 degrees) and 28 percent couldn't identify which way they were facing at all, 100 percent of Pormpuraawans could (Boroditsky & Gaby, 2010). Seeing as there is no evidence of any biological reason why these Aboriginal people would be so adept at orienting themselves with respect to geomagnetic directions, parsimony dictates that it must be language. These types of findings, though fascinating, may seem a far cry from a Western classroom, but in fact they are not.

Often times, the adults who constitute the "establishment" decry the music of youth as "too loud," "too provocative," or just "not music." A commonly heard refrain from today's older generation concerns the use of misogynistic terms by male rappers. One reason why the use of negative terms is seen as problematic has to do with the expectation that exposure to negative labels about women will affect how young boys think about and see females.

Although this hypothesis is consistent with both common sense and the studies we have just discussed, direct evidence to this end is only now beginning to emerge. One study that has directly examined the influence of rap songs on male perceptions of females did, in fact, find that after a single session of listening to a rap song with lyrics that are offensive to women, the males' perceptions of females became slightly more misogynistic (Cobb & Boettcher, 2007).

The aforementioned study found only a small, immediate effect (and the persistence of the misogynistic feelings was not assessed); however, it is reasonable to predict that with repeated exposure these effects may become even more pronounced. These results should help contextualize those of the Pormpuraawans: language does matter. For teachers, this certainly means that the specific language that they use must be carefully monitored. Equally important, however, is the need to monitor the language of students.

It should be noted that I am by no means advocating for widespread censorship, but I do think it is critically important that we are aware of the role that the labels we use to describe one another have on the world. Students who engage in misogynistic (or racist or homophobic, etc.) language need more than a reprimand or other punishment. The role that those labels play in their own assessment of the world should be examined. Is there a way to ask the student to think about the negative connotations of those labels? Have them consider how they would feel if a person were to call someone they love by a hurtful name. Essentially, take what may have become a habit or knee-jerk (i.e., the use of offensive language) response and actually examine it in a meaningful and explicit way.

COGNITION IN 160 CHARACTERS

With the affordability of so-called "smart" phones, the ability to send short message service (SMS) text messages (texts) has become so easy that they are practically a way of life nowadays. Because the length of a single text is limited to 160 characters, an entire sublanguage of *textisms* has developed. A simple truncation of an everyday word, such as "txt" for "text," is one form of textism that usually involves the disenvowelling of words.

Other forms include the use of alphanumeric blends to make words such as "gr8" for "great." And still others involve short abbreviations for multiple-word phrases, such as the more antiquated "lol" for "laugh out loud" or the more profane "stfu" for, well, I'll assume you know what that one is. The advantage of using textisms is that more thoughts can be sent within one text as the number of characters per "word" drops. Thus an entire conversation that might normally consist of as many as twenty words with well over 200 characters could be reduced to as few as six to eight textisms in less than 100 characters. And, of course, then there are the emoticons . . . ;).

Texting doesn't follow standard rules of English. Because of character limits, punctuation is often absent. Given the nature of textisms, many have wondered whether texting has a negative impact on (standard) language acquisition and usage. Some studies have found mixed results when examining texting behavior and writing or spelling (Plester, Wood, & Bell, 2008).

Several have found a relationship, with the number of texts sent by tweens being positively correlated with spelling accuracy (Plester, Wood, & Bell, 2008; Wood et al., 2011). However, those studies often use infrequent texters (little more than three texts per day) or children who had never texted prior to the study. Other studies which have examined behaviors related to the texting behaviors of older children who are more entrenched in their texting have found support for the hypothesis that texting negatively impacts skills associated with communicating in English, such as speaking, writing, and spelling.

In a sample of Australian adolescents, it was found that the use of textisms negatively related to both reading and spelling (De Jonge & Kemp, 2012). Furthermore, the frequent receiving and sending of texts (over 1,000/week or the equivalent of one every six minutes of a waking 16-hour day) was found to negatively impact students' ability to successfully use mnemonic strategies (Ryker, Viosca, Lawrence, & Kleen, 2011).

The researchers in that study hypothesized that because many mnemonics are similar to textisms (compare the three words of "lol" with the five Great Lakes of "homes"), heavy texters may be able to use mnemonic strategies to their advantage. However, their hypothesis was not supported. In fact, the opposite was found to be true: texting seemed to diminish the efficacy of mnemonic strategies.

Ryker and colleagues provide several suggestions to explain their results, including that texters may be desensitized to the power of mnemonics because of their frequent use of textisms, that there may be limits to one's mnemonic/texting vocabulary, and/or that frequent communication via text messaging may be altering the neural and cognitive processes that heavy texters use. Though there is little research to support any of these claims, data are beginning to emerge that support the argument that the brains of heavy texters do process linguistic information differently than those of light or non-texters (Berger & Coch, 2010).

Overall, the data are unfortunately beginning to support the assertion that not only is texting negatively impacting the learning, retention, and usage of standard English but it may also be doing so through modifications of neural circuitry. Furthermore, it has been established that texting (sending and receiving) in class leads to lower performance on class assessments (Clayson & Haley, 2013). So what is an instructor to do?

Many have outlawed the use of cell phones altogether in the classroom — a policy I have in my own courses. Some teachers have integrated texting into their curriculum as a means of increasing student engagement. This seems like a good plan provided that firm rules governing the structure of texts are put into place. Proper spelling and grammar should be required when using cell phones as educational tools. This will then challenge students to think succinctly. This may be more difficult than it seems as the 160-character limit will seem much more restrictive when a student has to contemplate how to express his/her thoughts using normally sized words and phrases.

Ultimately, research may yield insight into some heretofore unknown cognitive or academic benefits that are conferred upon those who text heavily. Perhaps there is a place for students who are used to living in a constant state of hyperawareness, waiting for their next message to magically appear.

POINTS TO REMEMBER:

- Some of our oldest memories are words that we use every day.
- Language consists of more than just speech. Hand gestures are necessary for normal levels of performance. Adding hand gestures may even enhance some learning.

- Gestures need to be easy to understand and should be based on movements that are naturally associated with what is being learned.
- Statements of negation and use of the passive voice both require more cognitive resources than positive statements and the active voice.
- Language learning is optimized when a person is physically present.
- Baby media does not help language development. Similarly, listening to classical music doesn't enhance cognition.
- Music instruction enhances auditory sensitivity and may have some benefits to other forms of cognition, such as spatial reasoning.
- Language influences how we think.
- Evidence suggests that texting has a negative impact on several cognitive processes, including attention, learning, writing, and speaking.

REFERENCES

Bangerter, A., & Heath, C. (2004). The Mozart effect: Tracking the evolution of a scientific legend. *British Journal of Social Psychology, 43*(4), 605–623.

Berger, N. I., & Coch, D. (2010). Do u txt? Event-related potentials to semantic anomalies in standard and texted English. *Brain and Language, 113*(3), 135–148.

Boroditsky, L., & Gaby, A. (2010). Remembrances of times east: Absolute spatial representations of time in an Australian Aboriginal community. *Psychological Science, 21*(11), 1635–1639.

Boroditsky, L., Fuhrman, O., & McCormick, K. (2011). Do English and Mandarin speakers think about time differently? *Cognition, 118*(1), 123–129.

Broaders, S. C., Cook, S. W., Mitchell, Z., & Goldin-Meadow, S. (2007). Making children gesture brings out implicit knowledge and leads to learning. *Journal of Experimental Psychology: General, 136*(4), 539–550.

Broca, P. (1861). Remarks on the seat of the faculty of articulated language, following an observation of aphemia (loss of speech). *Bulletin de la Société Anatomique, 6,* 330–357.

Clayson, D. E., & Haley, D. A. (2013). An introduction to multitasking and texting: Prevalence and impact on grades and GPA in marketing classes. *Journal of Marketing Education,* in press.

Cook, S. W., Mitchell, Z., & Goldin-Meadow, S. (2008). Gesturing makes learning last. *Cognition, 106*(2), 1047–1058.

Črnčec, R., Wilson, S. J., & Prior, M. (2006). The cognitive and academic benefits of music to children: Facts and fiction. *Educational Psychology, 26*(4), 579–594.

Cobb, M.D., & Boettcher, W.A. (2007). Ambivalent sexism and misogynistic rap music: does exposure to Eminem increase sexism? *Journal of Applied Social Psychology, 37*(12), 3025-3042.

de Gelder, B. (2006). Towards the neurobiology of emotional body language. *Nature Reviews Neuroscience, 7*(3), 242–249.

De Jonge, S., & Kemp, N. (2012). Text-message abbreviations and language skills in high school and university students. *Journal of Research in Reading, 35*(1), 49–68.

DeLoache, J. S., Chiong, C., Sherman, K., Islam, N., Vanderborght, M., Troseth, G. L., & O'Doherty, K. (2010). Do babies learn from baby media? *Psychological Science, 21*(11), 1570–1574.

Ferreira, F. (2003). The misinterpretation of noncanonical sentences. *Cognitive Psychology, 47*(2), 164–203.
Fogassi, L., & Ferrari, P. F. (2012). Cortical motor organization, mirror neurons, and embodied language: An evolutionary perspective. *Biolinguistics, 6*(3–4), 308–337.
Friederici, A. D. (2009). Pathways to language: Fiber tracts in the human brain. *Trends in Cognitive Sciences, 13*(4), 175–181.
Geschwind, N. (1965). Disconnexion syndromes in animals and man. Part I. *Brain, 88,* 237–294.
Hadar, U. (1989). Two types of gesture and their role in speech production. *Journal of Language and Social Psychology, 8,* 221–228.
Hannon, E. E., & Trainor, L. J. (2007). Music acquisition: Effects of enculturation and formal training on development. *Trends in Cognitive Sciences, 11*(11), 466–472.
Kelly, S. D., McDevitt, T., & Esch, M. (2009). Brief training with co-speech gesture lends a hand to word learning in a foreign language. *Language and Cognitive Processes, 24*(2), 313–334.
Khermouch, G. (Jan 11, 2004). Brainier babies? Maybe. Big sales? Definitely. *Bloomberg Businessweek Magazine.*
Kraus, N., & Chandrasekaran, B. (2010). Music training for the development of auditory skills. *Nature Reviews Neuroscience, 11*(8), 599–605.
Kuhl, P. K., Tsao, F. M., & Liu, H. M. (2003). Foreign-language experience in infancy: Effects of short-term exposure and social interaction on phonetic learning. *Proceedings of the National Academy of Sciences, 100*(15), 9096–9101.
Macedonia, M., & Knosche, T. R. (2011). Body in mind: How gestures empower foreign language learning. *Mind, Brain, and Education, 5*(4), 196–211.
McGregor, K. K., Rohlfing, K. J., Bean, A., & Marschner, E. (2009). Gesture as a support for word learning: The case of under. *Journal of Child Language, 36*(4), 807.
Menon, V., & Levitin, D. J. (2005). The rewards of music listening: Response and physiological connectivity of the mesolimbic system. *Neuroimage, 28*(1), 175–184.
Montgomery, K. J., Isenberg, N., & Haxby, J. V. (2007). Communicative hand gestures and object-directed hand movements activated the mirror neuron system. *Social Cognitive and Affective Neuroscience, 2*(2), 114–122.
Patel, A. D. (2003). Language, music, syntax and the brain. *Nature Neuroscience, 6*(7), 674–681.
Plester, B., Wood, C., & Bell, V. (2008). Txt msg n school literacy: Does texting and knowledge of text abbreviations adversely affect children's literacy attainment? *Literacy, 42*(3), 137–144.
Rauscher, F. H., Shaw, G. L., & Ky, K. N. (1993). Music and spatial task performance. *Nature, 365,* 611.
Rauscher, F. H., Krauss, R. M., & Chen, Y. (1996). Gesture, speech, and lexical access: The role of lexical movements in speech production. *Psychological Science, 7*(4), 226–231.
Rauscher, F. H., & Hinton, S. C. (2006). The Mozart effect: Music listening is not music instruction. *Educational Psychologist, 41*(4), 233–238.
Regier, T., & Kay, P. (2009). Language, thought, and color: Whorf was half right. *Trends in Cognitive Sciences, 13*(10), 439–446.
Rekart, J. L., & Routtenberg, A. (2008). Post-translational brain protein modification as substrate for memories that last a lifetime. *BioTech International, 20*(5), 6–8.
Robb, M., Richert, R., & Wartella, E. (2009). Just a talking book? Word learning from watching baby videos. *British Journal of Developmental Psychology, 27,* 27–45.
Ryker, R. E., Viosca, C., Lawrence, S., & Kleen, B. (2011). Texting and the efficacy of mnemonics: Is too much texting detrimental? *Information Systems Education Journal, 9*(2), 27.
Sack, K. (1998, January 15). Georgia's governor seeks musical start for babies. *The New York Times,* A-12.
Schellenberg, E. G. (2004). Music lessons enhance IQ. *Psychological Science, 15*(8), 511–514.

Sparks, S. D. (2011). Schools "flip" for lesson model promoted by Khan Academy. *Education Week, 31*(5), 1–14.

Steele, K. M., Bass, K. E., & Crook, M. D. (1999). The mystery of the Mozart effect: Failure to replicate. *Psychological Science, 10*(4), 366–369.

Valenzeno, L., Alibali, M. W., & Klatzky, R. (2003). Teachers' gestures facilitate students' learning: A lesson in symmetry. *Contemporary Educational Psychology, 28*(2), 187–204.

Wason, P. C. (1959). The processing of positive and negative information. *Quarterly Journal of Experimental Psychology, 11*(2), 92–107.

Wernicke, C. (1874). *Der aphasiche Symptomenkomplex.* Breslau, Poland: Cohen and Weigert.

Whorf, B. L. (1940). Science and linguistics. *Technological Review, 44,* 229–231, 247–248.

Wood, C., Meachem, S., Bowyer, S., Jackson, E., Tarczynski-Bowles, M. L., & Plester, B. (2011). A longitudinal study of children's text messaging and literacy development. *British Journal of Psychology, 102*(3), 431–442.

Zimmerman, F. J., Christakis, D. A., & Meltzoff, A. (2007). Television and DVD/video viewing in children younger than 2 years. *Archives of Pediatric & Adolescent Medicine, 69,* 473–479.

EIGHT
Decision Making

We like to believe that we are masters of our own destiny—captains of our own ships—however, this belief fails to consider that the ways in which our minds make many decisions are actually influenced by a predictable number of factors. Though on the surface decision making in general may seem like a broad topic, we will be able to readily restrict our discussion of it to education and classroom practice.

For example, decisions between two choices, such as should I continue studying or quit, are influenced by motivation. We will examine which factors and techniques are evidence-based and which are not. Furthermore, we will delve, to some extent, into the psychological literature on consumer behavior and may even be surprised at the ways that the tips and tools of marketers can be put to pedagogical advantage.

BASICS OF DECISION MAKING

Not all decisions are made under the same sets of circumstances. Some decisions, those for which we know with no doubt what the outcomes will be, are *decisions under certainty*. For example, if I decide to throw a ball up in the air so that I may catch it, I have little doubt about the laws of physics. If, however, we are unsure as to what might happen but have an accurate sense of the likelihood of different outcomes, then we are making a *decision under risk*.

The key to decisions under risk is that the odds are accurately known. Thus for one to make a decision under risk means the specific probability must be known. For example, if I opt to buy a multi-state lottery ticket (such as Powerball), I decide that the money (one or two dollars) I am risking is worth the chance, no matter how remote (and remote it is, usually on the order of 1 in 175,000,000) the chance of winning tens or even hundreds of millions of dollars is. Notice, for a decision under risk to be made, the likelihood of a preferred outcome doesn't have to be great or even likely; it just has to be known.

On the other hand, there are many circumstances in life in which we don't know the actual probabilities that predict the ramifications of our decisions. It is these *decisions under ambiguity* (or *uncertainty*) that are perhaps the most interesting of the three to study. Why are they the most intriguing? They are the most intriguing because individuals, though they don't know the actual probability or odds, make decisions as though they *do* (Ellsberg, 1961).

It is these types of decisions that are also germane to our treatment of pedagogical applications of cognitive psychological research because decisions such as (1) should I study more (or at all), (2) do I go to college, and, if so, (3) for what are all decisions for which precise statistical probabilities are not available. For example, we do not know when we study for an exam if an extra 15 minutes of review will have a 65 percent chance of increasing our grade by five points or more. Indeed, we don't even know if it will help at all. We believe (and hope) that it will and base our decision on rules of thumb (e.g., more studying = better grades), but in the end, there is still uncertainty.

Most individuals dislike ambiguity and will select options that have known probabilities over those with unknown. This situation is somewhat intriguing because the ambiguous options could, in fact, be more likely than the risky situation. Consider a situation in which there are two bags of jelly beans. In the first bag, it is known that there are 20 cherry flavored and ten black licorice flavored.

There are also 30 total jelly beans in a second bag; however, the only information available about that bag is that it contains both cherry and black licorice jelly beans; the exact number of each type is unknown. Now, let's assume that a child absolutely despises black licorice but really would like a jelly bean, which bag is she most likely to take a jelly bean from, assuming that she is not allowed to look first?

Studies have shown that in this situation the child will almost definitely opt for the first bag with the known 2:1 ratio of cherry to black licorice flavors, despite the fact that the second bag could contain only 3 black licorice (at a ratio of 9:1; Hsu et al., 2005). It is believed that the second bag is eschewed for the first because on the whole humans are *risk averse* (Loewenstein & Hsee, 2001). Risk aversion is most often seen when gains are involved as illustrated in the following example.

A radio station has a game whereby the eighth caller, after successfully answering a question, will have the opportunity to win cash. The eighth caller is selected, correctly answers the question, "What Grateful Dead song mentions the four winds?," and then is presented with the following scenario:

The caller may opt to win $100 for correctly answering the question ("Franklin's Tower") or may instead have a coin tossed and if it comes up heads, she will win $200.

So what will the caller do? What would you do? Chances are excellent that the caller (and you) will choose the $100 over the gamble. What is striking about this choice is that mathematically both options are exactly the same. To see this, we first have to consider the total possible value for each option, which is called *expected utility*. The expected utility is calculated by taking the product of the odds of any outcome times the actual value of that outcome.

For the first option, there is a probability of one (out of one) times $100, which gives an expected utility of $100. Written out, the equation would look like this:

$$\text{Expected utility 1} = 1\ (\$100) = \$100$$

And for the second option, the one with the gamble, the expected utility can be calculated using the same equation, in which one out of every two flips (0.5 likelihood) may result in $200 and one out of every two flips will yield nothing (0.5 likelihood):

$$\text{Expected utility 2} = 0.5\ (\$200) + 0.5\ (\$0) = \$100$$

As can be seen, the expected utility of both options is identical. Thus risk aversion is not about logic or statistics. Though a choice is made by individuals, it is done without regard for the statistics of the situation. For if the probabilities of each outcome were the driving force, we would be unable to choose. The inability to make a decision when two equally tantalizing and indiscernibly similar options are available is best illustrated by the example of Buridan's donkey (OK, so technically it was Buridan's "ass," but we're trying to keep this book G-rated).

The animal in this fable was starving and placed between two equally large bales of hay. However, despite the animal's overwhelming hunger, it eventually starved to death. Why? The two bales of hay were each the same distance from the animal. Because the cost (distance to travel) and reward (amount of hay) for each bale was exactly the same, there was no *rational* reason for the donkey to select one over the other, and thus it died (Cook & Levi, 1990). Luckily, many of our decisions, unlike Buridan's mythical donkey, are *not* grounded in rational comparisons between options; we would just select one of the bales.

THE DECISION-MAKING TOOLBOX: HEURISTICS AND ALGORITHMS

When one is confronted with a choice point that requires a decision, like which bale of hay or bag of jelly beans, s/he has two mechanisms available to make a decision. The first is to examine all of the data and information available exhaustively until the one, correct decision is selected. If we engaged in this process of systematically weighing all available options and contingencies and weighting each one according to various criteria, such as money, time expenditure, and so forth, we would be using an *algorithm*.

If, on the other hand, we decided to forego all of the time needed to explore all possibilities, then we would use a *heuristic*. Unlike algorithms, heuristics reduce effort and/or ignore some of the information that is available (Shah & Oppenheimer, 2008). Heuristics, which are often referred to as "rules of thumb," are used because they conserve mental effort (i.e., attention and working memory) for other tasks.

However, because not all available information is used, and instead past experiences are used as stand-ins for current data, heuristics have a lower probability of leading to the best choice. Heuristics are used all the time and with great success; however, when a new situation doesn't quite fit the experiences and examples upon which heuristics are built, the decision that we make can be less than ideal.

DECISION MAKING AND THE BRAIN

As may be expected, different systems within the brain are responsible for different types of decisions. Over the past decade, there has been increased attention to the manner in which different patterns of brain activation correspond to decisions made under differing circumstances. When emotions are involved in decision making, such as by displaying risk aversion when gains are involved, the amygdala is strongly associated.

Interestingly, when emotionality is tempered, as may occur when rationality needs to take over (say when the odds of a gain occurring are so small that ambiguity is the better choice), areas of the frontal lobes, such as the medial orbitofrontal cortex, are activated. These findings indicate that other parts of the brain must be activated so as to override emotional centers, such as the amygdala, in order to make some types of decisions (DeMartino, Kumaran, Seymour, & Dolan, 2006).

Interestingly, this overriding of behavior may be due to the role that the orbitofrontal cortex plays in our feelings of *regret*, which are defined as negative feelings associated with a poor decision (Coricelli, Dolan, & Sirigu, 2007). Thus it is because we consider how we might feel if we were not to have a gain that we make certain decisions. Other regions of the brain that also underlie various types of decision making include the striatum, the anterior cingulate cortex, the prefrontal cortex, and the insula (Rangel, Camerer, & Montague, 2008).

EMOTIONAL CHOICES

Risk aversion, as already touched upon, results from a desire to avoid regret. The ways in which risks are assessed depend, in part, upon when the potential reward is believed to be delivered. When rewards are imminent, the so-called "emotional" areas of the brain, under the direct control of the dopaminergic system (which is responsible for our feelings of pleasure, as well as addictive behaviors; Hyman, Malenka, & Nestler, 2006), such as the striatum, are activated.

If, however, there is a delay between the decision and the actual payoff, then the prefrontal and parietal cortices display much higher activation (McClure, Laibson, Loewenstein, & Cohen, 2004). The broad interpretation of these findings is that when the outcome of a decision won't be enjoyed or fully realized until later, we use what may be considered more "rational" parts of the brain. If, however, we are forced to make a judgment or decision that will have a payoff or penalty immediately, then emotional centers of the brain call the shots.

For years, high-pressure sales tactics have utilized cognitive psychological techniques to get people to make purchases that, given some time and space, they may not have otherwise made. Then, because individuals don't like to consider the fact that they may have been had or perhaps paid more than they could (or should) have, they will convince themselves that they got a good deal after all. These two separate though related phenomena, *emotional decision making* and *cognitive dissonance*, are as useful for the educator as they are for the used-car salesman.

Cognitive dissonance was first described by Festinger in 1957. This concept is often used to explain what happens when we modify reality within our minds to try to rationalize a decision or a belief. We do this, as described previously, to make it seem OK that we spent a little bit more on a car than we originally budgeted. It also occurs when we change our impression or knowledge about someone or something rather than change a preexisting belief of ours.

Cognitive dissonance arises when we have a lack of a match between something we believe and something that we experience. In order to resolve the internal struggle that then takes place, we often times change our recollection or perspective of the experience so that it better matches our beliefs.

Vanessa has received a grade of "D" on an examination for which she maintains that she studied quite hard. Her below-average grade (experience) is inconsistent with her own belief about her behavior (studious and diligent). Per Festinger (and numerous others over the last half-century), Vanessa will need to resolve this disequilibrium or dissonance in one of two ways.

Ideally, she would acknowledge that there is something wrong with the way that she studies and resolve to seek help or try a different set of studying strategies. However, she may also, and we have all encountered students who do this, resolve the dissonance by failing to take responsibility for her poor performance (e.g., Gosling, Denizeau, & Oberlé, 2006). This resolution of the shame or guilt felt by the student is thus resolved by blaming the test for not covering the proper material, being "unfair," not being properly prepared by the instructor, or any number of other rationalizations. It is this latter situation which creates problems within the classroom as well as for the student's long-term success.

Cognitive dissonance is a powerful motivator, one that has even been put on par with biological drivers of behavior, such as hunger (Festinger, 1957). So how can an instructor avoid dissonance, or, perhaps more realistically, help redirect students who engage in it? In this circumstance, it should first be noted that the likelihood of the student just "owning up" to not really studying is not good.

The motivation to relieve shame over not doing well will not be overcome by making the student feel further *additional* shame for not taking responsibility. Indeed, cognitive dissonance tells us that the opposite will happen and the student will become even more entrenched in her stance that the problem with her test resides with factors not related to her. What is necessary in this situation is to echo that the student is not happy with her performance and to suggest solutions that may enhance performance on future exams.

Rather than trying to move her from her belief about the recent examination, the proposed interaction works to facilitate future success without engaging in a confrontational tête-à-tête that may do damage to the student:teacher dynamic.

IT'S ALL ABOUT CONTEXT

How much would you rather spend for a book: $20 or $19.99? Though the answer as to why you would choose to save a cent may seem obvious, the reason why retailers have settled upon the "as seen on TV" price of 19 dollars and 99 cents may not be. Before we delve into the "why," let's examine another hypothetical situation, but in this case, instead of books, let's talk real estate.

A hypothetical realtor has three homes for sale in three different but comparable neighborhoods. All have the same number of bedrooms, bathrooms, square footage, lot size, amenities, and so forth. The only notable difference, other than paint choices, between the three is the price. Those prices are:

Home #1: $240,000
Home #2: $239,900
Home #3: $239,000

Remember that for all intents and purposes, these homes are the same. Now, all things being equal, which home will likely fetch an offer that is closest to the list price? On the surface, we might think that it is Home #3, as it is the cheapest. However, this is not necessarily the case.

All things being equal, Home #2 will land the sellers a final sale that is closer to their asking price than either Home #1 or #3, and thus will most likely net the largest overall sale. It isn't that the $100 savings (between #1 and #2) is too great a deal to pass up because #3 has a ten-fold greater ($1000) savings. In this case, what will happen is that the original price tag of each of these homes sets the context for future negotiations.

Examine what it looks like when we write out exactly how we would *think* about these three home prices in our minds:

Home #1: Two hundred and forty *thousand* dollars
Home #2: Two hundred and thirty-nine thousand, nine *hundred* dollars
Home #3: Two hundred and thirty-nine *thousand* dollars

The last dollar amount for Home #2, unlike #1 or #3, is in hundreds of dollars and not thousands. Because of this difference, when we begin negotiating prices, we will reduce the price by less if we think of it in hundreds rather than thousands of dollars. The same goes for our "As seen on TV" book for $19.99 from the start of this section. Because it finishes with cents rather than dollars, it doesn't *feel* as though it as expensive as a $20 book. Put differently, when we *don't* think about it, that one cent does much more than just add a hundredth of a dollar to the total cost, it actually completely reframes how we think about it.

This phenomenon, called *semantic framing*, is used all the time in marketing and extends beyond the actual dollar or cents. There is a reason that ground meat is sold in terms of the percentage lean rather than the percentage fat (e.g., 93% lean). Namely, because more people will buy a food if it is framed in terms of something that most of us (rightly) believe to be healthy, which, in this case, is lean (rather than fatty) meat.

Knowledge of semantic framing is of as much importance to education as it is to marketing. First, always be sure to think through how you are going to frame statements to students and classes. If you are trying to motivate a student who is a bit down about his performance on a 100-question exam, then you might tell him "Let's focus on the fact that you did get 70 questions correct!" and not "Let's focus on the fact that you only missed 30 questions." From a cognitive standpoint, the word "only" in this and similar cases is useless. Qualifying words that are supposed to be reassuring like "only," "just," and so forth don't offset the semantic framing of negativity that is evoked by words like "missed," "lost," or "incorrect."

Second, we have to be cautious about misrepresenting certainty when it is not present. For example, I have yet to see a commercial where it is mentioned that five out of five dentists prefer (insert any brand name you desire here) toothpaste. Though there is a lack of unanimity, marketers still want you to know that 4 out of 5 (or even 3) *dentists* prefer this brand of toothpaste. In this case, the concept of "dentist" as an expert is what is selling the product; the specific number is less relevant.

The influence of so-called experts on our decisions also hold true for education. Research has demonstrated that the general public is more willing to accept a myth about behavior or the brain as being true if the prefix neuro- is used or if it is suggested that neuroscientific, neurological, or some other form of brain research has "proven"[1] it to be true. Indeed, over the past quarter-century, the term "brain-based" has been put to good use to market to educators and the lay public any number of different texts, workbooks, software, techniques, and manuals. Though many of these products are perfectly fine, the fact that the term "brain" helped to sell them shouldn't be ignored.

The inclusion of images of brain activity makes explanations of cognition seem more plausible. McCabe and Castel (2008) found that when images of brain activity accompanied descriptions of findings that were slightly outlandish (i.e., TV watching related to mathematical ability) or from actual articles, the scientific reasoning of the articles was enhanced by the images. These results are similar to those of Weisberg and colleagues who found that poor scientific explanations for behavior were more readily accepted if neuroscientific terms or explanations were included (Weisberg, Keil, Goodstein, & Rawson, 2008).

Taken together, these findings speak to the importance of appropriately contextualizing scientific data for students, so as to ensure that nuance and objective problems with studies or their findings are not dismissed because of the terms or images that accompany them. Furthermore, educators themselves need to be aware of these findings so that they do not fall privy to the perpetuation of many of the persistent brain-related myths (neuromyths; see chapter 1) that pervade the field of education today.

Thus whether we are in front of a group of students or speaking one-on-one with a parent, we must be cautious about what we label as being "supported by research," "best practice," and "evidence-based." If the label actually fits and we are certain of our knowledge (i.e., it has support outside our own experience), then that is fine. However, there have been occasions when something that is believed to be a "best practice" is found to be no better than other practices (a *"neither best nor worst practice"* perhaps).

Findings that may be ambiguous in nature, meaning not strongly predictive or dismissive of a particular hypothesis, have been shown to be interpreted by individuals as supportive of their own beliefs. Put differently, people will use vague findings, particularly those that have the "seal of approval" of "scientific evidence" to support their own beliefs, despite the fact that the actual findings (or even the authors of the study) make no such claim (Bastardi, Uhlmann, & Ross, 2011).

DECISION MAKING AND MOTIVATION

All decisions aren't equal. Some we launch into head-first with great enthusiasm. With others, we hem and haw, sit on the fence, and, finally, make a selection. One of the differences between these two scenarios is motivation. Motivation is an important affective (i.e., related to emotions) component of decision making and one that we will consider here.

Instructor feedback is viewed as being a critical component of the teaching:learning dyad. But do teacher comments actually facilitate academic success? In a landmark study, Page examined how teacher comments affected performance. Over 2,000 students in 74 classrooms were given either: (1) generic feedback that all students receiving the same grade would receive, (2) specific feedback that was individualized to each student's performance, or (3) no feedback (1958).

After the comments were given, performance on the next examination was then compared among the three groups. It was found that as long as comments were received by the student (i.e., both generic and custom), performance on the following exam was enhanced.

However, subsequent attempts to replicate these results have had mixed findings, with some failing (Stewart & White, 1976) and others successfully finding a feedback effect (Olina & Sullivan, 2002). In practice, some researchers may find a negligible effect of teacher comments on performance because of the types of comments, the perceived applicability of the comments to the given student, and the existing relationship between the teacher and student.

It does seem safe to speculate that praise, when specifically and directly focused at particular students, does, in fact, lead to increases in motivation, that then subsequently affects learning in a positive manner (Black & William, 2006).

Sometimes what is motivating doesn't have anything to do with emotion on the surface. Consider two students: Tim and Tyson. Tim has just scored a 91 on an exam while Tyson achieved an 89. Though numerically only two percentage points separate the two individuals, it turns out that in terms of motivation the rift may as well be miles apart. Because Tyson just missed the cutoff for an A, he will be more motivated to do better (including presumably studying more or more efficiently) for the next exam than will Tim, for whom a 91 is absolutely fine.

All things being equal, it is the "round" score of "90" that is the difference between our two hypothetical students. Research has shown that when individuals score just below a round number, as was the case with our 89, the near miss acts to motivate individuals to do better (or request a retake). On the other hand, when a round number has just been exceeded, as was the case with our 91, the performance is actually *de-motivating* (Pope & Simonsohn, 2011).

Because many aspects of grading are, by their very nature, subjective, many teachers feel as though "effort" should be factored into scores. Usually, such "effort" adjustments result in a slight push from one grade, often times below a round number, to a slightly higher one. The idea behind the "nudge" is that the extra few points (or jump in a letter grade) will reward the student for her diligence and will motivate her to do better in the future. Data such as those generated by studies akin to Pope and Simonsohn should give the well-intentioned teacher pause before "bumping up" any grades.

The life of an educator is one of constant instructing, assigning, and grading. It turns out that the timeline associated with this last piece, grading, can have an impact upon one's performance on an assignment. Disappointment, like many negative feelings, is one that we like to put off for as long as possible. It turns out that when we are able to stave off possible disappointment, we are less motivated to do our best.

Kettle and Häubl (2010) showed that individual performance was maximized when participants believed that they would receive feedback sooner rather than later. The researchers hypothesized that the reason for this *proximate-feedback effect* was due, at least in part, to the fact that when we believe we will be judged in the near future, the possibility of being disappointed by someone's judgment motivates us to do slightly better. Put differently, the threat of disappointment is more *real* when we think it may be coming soon rather than at some abstract time in the future.

This explanation is consistent with the fact that (1) humans have a poor sense of time and the future (see chapter 2 on the perception of time) and (2) when we make decisions that relate to short-term goals, the emotional parts of our brain are more active than they are when we make longer-term decisions. In this context, finding out one's grade tomorrow rather than next week causes the negative grade to be feared more and spurs one on to do his or her best (or at least a *little* better).

Though probably not a large effect when spread out over a reasonable period of time—like a day—whenever possible, it should be made explicitly clear to students that feedback on their work will be swift (and specifically and sufficiently detailed; see previous discussion).

DECISION MAKING AND ... SANDWICHES?

We've talked about a number of factors that all intuitively relate to one's ability to make decisions, including emotions, how information is framed, feedback (both content and timing), and our own self-protection. However, what about factors that are seemingly unrelated, yet can have a serious impact upon our choices?

In a phenomenally well done and disturbing study, Danzinger and colleagues (2011) examined how the time of day affected the parole decisions of Israeli judges. The researchers in this study exploited the fact that in the Israeli judicial system, there are two well-structured food breaks that take place.

By examining whether parole was granted or denied across the course of the day, the researchers were able to determine whether different factors may unknowingly influence the parole decisions of jurists. Though nearly 65 percent of rulings that took place first thing in the morning were favorable for the prisoner (i.e., parole granted), this percentage dropped down to nearly zero right before the scheduled food break. Then after each break, the percentage jumped back up to 65 percent again. The same pattern was seen directly before and after each of the parole board's breaks for the food.

Given the seriousness of these findings, the researchers examined several possible mitigating factors. For example, it was examined whether the most serious offenders were seen by the parole board directly before lunch and this was why so few of those inmates were granted parole; however, no relationship was found between when the prisoner went before the board (ordinal position; 1st, 3rd, etc.) and the sentence that was delivered.

Relationships also were not found between judgments and the number of previous incarcerations, the number of months served, or whether the prisoner was actively involved in some form of rehabilitation. The only factor that reliably determined whether the prisoner would receive a favorable ruling was how soon before or after the parole board's break for food that individual was seen.

These findings are directly applicable to the types of judgments and decisions made by educators. Though not making decisions about whether to allow people to reenter society, teachers do decide what grades to assign to projects, papers, and examinations. Though not an issue for objective, multiple-choice-type tests, even the best-designed rubrics for other types of assessments still allow for some interpretation and "gray areas."

As many educators know, the grading of papers is often (dare I write, primarily) conducted at home, after the school day has terminated. It is important that educators are cognizant of the non-performance factors that can affect the grades assigned to students, such as whether the grader in question is hungry or not. It is hoped that this is not seen as a trivial point; the article that was discussed speaks of the importance of being aware of one's own level of fatigue and hunger. Though not a matter of prison vs. no prison, when it comes to grading, there are a sufficient number of subjective factors at play and to introduce more is problematic and not fair to the students.

Care should be taken that if hunger strikes, perhaps the papers should be put on hold until after a snack. Additionally, these findings suggest against organizing papers alphabetically before grading (to facilitate later entry into a gradebook), as by the end of a grading session, there may be small penalties that students with names beginning with "R" are assessed that students with "A" names were not. If papers are always organized in this fashion, then these small penalties could compound over the course of a semester or year into a significant reduction of students' grades.

POINTS TO REMEMBER

- There are three types of decisions: those for which the outcome of a decision is known, those for which the likelihood of outcomes is known, and those for which there is no information about the exact probability of an outcome.
- Most people prefer choices where they know the odds over choices with ambiguous outcomes.
- When there is a possibility of a decision leading to some kind of a gain (points awarded, money, etc.), people tend to be risk averse.
- Algorithms are formulaic, step-by-step mechanisms that can be used to solve problems. To save time and energy, often times heuristics, which are rules of thumb, are used instead of algorithms.
- Many decisions are made to avoid feeling regret over what might have been.
- Cognitive dissonance is a powerful motivator that affects our decisions. Cognitive dissonance occurs when our beliefs and reality do not align. One way we resolve this dissonance is by modifying our perceptions of a situation to more closely match our beliefs.
- Semantic framing refers to the way that decisions are affected by the way in which choices are presented.
- Statements can be made to seem more believable or valid by adding expert testimony, scientific images, or the use of scientific vernacular, particularly when it refers to the brain.
- Feedback should be provided as soon as possible in order to tap into the positive effect of proximate feedback upon performance.
- People strive for round numbers, particularly multiples of 10. Individuals who score just below a round number will see a motiva-

tional boost to their efforts and those who score just above will see a motivational decrement.
- Important decisions can be affected by a number of physiological factors, including hunger and fatigue.

NOTE

1. It should be noted that the goal of science is not to "prove" anything but rather to falsify competing hypotheses.

REFERENCES

Airasian, P. W., & Jones, A. M. (1993). The teacher as applied measurer: Realities of classroom measurement and assessment. *Applied Measurement in Education, 6*(3), 241–254.

Bastardi, A., Uhlmann, E. L., & Ross, L. (2011). Wishful thinking: Belief, desire, and the motivated evaluation of scientific evidence. *Psychological Science, 22*(6), 731–732.

Black, P., & Wiliam, D. (2006) Developing a theory of formative assessment. In J. Gardner (Ed.), *Assessment and learning* (pp. 81–100). London: Sage.

Cook, K. S., & Levi, M. (Eds.). (1990). *The limits of rationality*. Chicago: University of Chicago Press.

Coricelli, G., Dolan, R. J., & Sirigu, A. (2007). Brain, emotion and decision making: The paradigmatic example of regret. *Trends in Cognitive Sciences, 11*(6), 258–265.

Danziger, S., Levav, J., & Avnaim-Pesso, L. (2011). Extraneous factors in judicial decisions. *Proceedings of the National Academy of Sciences, 108*(17), 6889–6892.

De Martino, B., Kumaran, D., Seymour, B., & Dolan, R. J. (2006). Frames, biases, and rational decision-making in the human brain. *Science, 313*(5787), 684–687.

Ellsberg, D. (1961). Risk, ambiguity, and the Savage axioms. *The Quarterly Journal of Economics, 4*(75), 643–669.

Festinger, L. (1957). *A theory of cognitive dissonance*. Stanford, CA: Stanford University Press.

Gosling, P., Denizeau, M., & Oberlé, D. (2006). Denial of responsibility: A new mode of dissonance reduction. *Journal of Personality and Social Psychology, 90*, 722–733.

Hsu, M., Bhatt, M., Adolphs, R., Tranel, D., & Camerer, C. F. (2005). Neural systems responding to degrees of uncertainty in human decision-making. *Science, 310*(5754), 1680–1683.

Hyman, S. E., Malenka, R. C., & Nestler, E. J. (2006). Neural mechanisms of addiction: The role of reward-related learning and memory. *Annu. Rev. Neurosci., 29*, 565–598.

Kettle, K. L., & Häubl, G. (2010). Motivation by anticipation expecting rapid feedback enhances performance. *Psychological Science, 21*(4), 545–547.

Loewenstein, G. F., & Hsee, C. K. (2001). Risk as feelings. *Psychological Bulletin, 127*(2), 267–286.

McCabe, D. P., & Castel, A. D. (2008). Seeing is believing: The effect of brain images on judgments of scientific reasoning. *Cognition, 107*(1), 343–352.

McClure, S. M., Laibson, D. I., Loewenstein, G., & Cohen, J. D. (2004). Separate neural systems value immediate and delayed monetary rewards. *Science, 306*(5695), 503–507.

Olina, Z., & Sullivan, H. J. (2002). Effects of classroom evaluation strategies on student achievement and attitudes. *Educational Technology Research and Development, 50*(3), 61–75.

Page, E. B. (1958). Teacher comments and student performance: A seventy-four classroom experiment in school motivation. *Journal of Educational Psychology, 49*(4), 173–181.

Pope, D., & Simonsohn, U. (2011). Round numbers as goals evidence from baseball, SAT takers, and the lab. *Psychological Science, 22*(1), 71–79.

Rangel, A., Camerer, C., & Montague, P. R. (2008). A framework for studying the neurobiology of value-based decision making. *Nature Reviews Neuroscience, 9*(7), 545–556.

Shah A. K., & Oppenheimer, D. M. (2008). Heuristics made easy: An effort-reduction framework. *Psychological Bulletin, 137*, 207–222.

Stewart, L. G., & White, M. A. (1976). Teacher comments, letter grades, and student performance: What do we really know? *Journal of Educational Psychology, 68*(4), 488–500.

Weisberg, D. S., Keil, F. C., Goodstein, J., Rawson, E., & Gray, J. R. (2008). The seductive allure of neuroscience explanations. *Journal of Cognitive Neuroscience, 20*(3), 470–477.

NINE
Problem Solving

One purpose of formal schooling is to pass along critical knowledge and skills to the next generation. Though memorization of facts and concepts provides a foundation upon which higher-order thinking may be built, most teachers will tell you that what they actually want to develop in their students is critical reasoning skills. Reasoning is a higher-order skill, whereby existing knowledge is used to think about and solve problems. Problem solving relies on all of the cognitive processes that we have discussed to this point: perception, attention, working memory, long-term learning and memory, language, and decision making. Therefore the factors that affect each of those foundational skills will also affect problem solving. In this chapter, we will briefly touch upon some of the ways in which problems are solved and factors that can affect problem solving. In addition, we will examine what research tells us about creativity and how it may be facilitated.

TYPES OF PROBLEM SOLVING

Broadly speaking, there are two types of problem solving. The first, *directed thinking*, involves a conscious allocation of resources with the sole purpose of finding a solution. This form of thinking is what we most often think of when we use terms like "concentrate" or "focus" that speak to the distribution of attentional resources (see chapter 3). The second, *indirect thinking*, is what we associate with both daydreaming and creative insight; namely, the thinking that takes place on its own, without our guidance.

If you have ever sat through a meeting during which most of your time was spent on non-work related thoughts, that would be an example of indirect thinking. Similarly, if an answer to a question literally pops into your mind, even though you stopped consciously thinking about the problem, that would be another example of indirect thinking.

It is important to differentiate between these two types of thinking because to some extent they rely on different brain regions and are optimized using different strategies and techniques. Problem solving, the act of bringing together one's knowledge of skills and concepts to find the one correct answer, has been termed *convergent* thinking (Guilford, 1967). *Divergent* thought, on the other hand, is one's ability to go outside what one knows to find novel paths to any number of multiple solutions.

Divergent thinking may be of use when there isn't one clear solution or goal state for a problem. Problems for which there is a lack of clarity regarding the nature of the solution or the processes for arriving at a solution are referred to as *ill-defined*. Well-defined problems, on the other hand, have well-articulated initial states (we know what we are starting with), goal states (we know what the solution should look like), and operators (the behaviors or rules necessary to move from the initial state to the goal). Thus being told to paint a picture is an ill-defined problem because we don't know what the end product should be.

If I am to paint a picture, I need to arrive at an idea for a goal state on my own. In order to arrive at a decision, I'll likely consider several options. I could ask myself: "Should I paint a landscape?"; "Should there be trees (and should they be happy)?"; "Are we going to paint a landscape at all?"; "What about a portrait?" Contrast this with a different set of directions for this artistic endeavor: "paint a still life of this bowl of fruit that is on the center table." In this latter case, the end product is known.

Though the end state of a well-defined problem may be known, it doesn't mean that the solution is any easier to obtain. The game of chess has a well-defined goal state, *checkmate*; however, getting there can be quite challenging. The same applies to mathematical problem solving, where an equation and the rules for conducting arithmetic calculations are all well-defined, however, actually implementing the operators to successfully find a solution can prove to be challenging.

PROBLEM SOLVING, CREATIVITY, AND THE BRAIN

Convergent thinking in everyday life relies on several distinct neural systems. In general, the brain will defer to experience when attempting to solve problems using visual and spatial templates. The use of knowledge to solve problems is mediated by left temporal regions, whereas when rules are used to solve problems, absent of any context, both parietal lobes are recruited (Goel, Buchel, Frith, & Dolan, 2000; Goel & Dolan, 2003).

Often times problem solving involves overcoming what we might believe about the world (e.g., stereotypes) to see logical consistencies and inconsistencies. Because humans by default rely upon experience to make judgments, additional brain regions must be recruited when we need to see past our own beliefs. The left temporal lobe is actually inhibited by the dorsolateral prefrontal cortex when we must "suspend belief" in order to solve a problem. In contrast, when emotion intervenes and we make illogical choices, it is likely the result of activity within the ventromedial prefrontal cortex (Goel & Dolan, 2003).

Successful divergent thought relies on the ability to look at problems from unique perspectives. The neurological basis of this ability may be related not to activity in one brain region per se but rather to the *connectivity* between multiple brain regions. Remember that what we refer to as neurological connectivity is a byproduct of the number, strength, and distribution of white matter tracts laid down by axons linking one brain structure to another (chapter 1).

The largest bundle of white matter fibers (i.e., axons) in the brain is the corpus callosum, which coordinates activity between the left and right hemispheres of the brain. The corpus callosum may be critical to creativity because it provides the means for bringing together information that is processed differently by the two hemispheres (Heilman, Nadeau, & Beversdorf, 2003).

In fact, studies linking the size (Takeuchi, Taki, Sassa, Hashizume, Sekiguchi, Fukushima, & Kawashima, 2010) and activity (Takeuchi, Taki, Hashizume, Nagase, Nouchi, & Kawashima, 2012) of the white matter bundles, such as the corpus callosum, that link together the right and left prefrontal cortex and the temporal and parietal cortices are highly suggestive that it is the efficient binding of information processed in disparate brain regions that underlies creativity (Moore, Bhadelia, Billings, Fulwiler, Heilman, Rood, & Gansler, 2009). This cross-hemispheric linking may then lead to the greater synchronization of activity between the two hemispheres that is seen with divergent rather than convergent thinking (Jausovec & Jausovec, 2000).

Interestingly, the belief that left-handed people are more creative than right-handed may be a byproduct of the fact that left-handed individuals, on average, have larger corpus callosums than right-handed individuals (Witelson, 1985). If this is true, then thinking outside the box is due to the connections between the right and left hemisphere and not just being "right-brained" (which could be assumed because left-handers have a dominant right hemispheric motor cortex).

Indeed, after an extensive literature review of the plethora of studies using brain waves and neuroimaging to understand creativity, Dietrich and Kanso (2010) concluded that there is no research basis to suggest that either the right hemisphere is responsible for creativity or that so-called "right-brained" individuals are more creative.

PROBLEM-SOLVING STRATEGIES: HEURISTICS AND ALGORITHMS

Heuristics play a key role in problem solving, just as they did with decision making (see chapter 8). Remember, our minds evolved to use as few resources as necessary to get us through the day alive. Heuristics balance accuracy with efficiency; however, as we saw in chapter 7, they can break down when situations do not fit with the template needed for the heuristic to work.

As an example, let's work through a few anagrams. As a reminder, an anagram contains all of the letters of a word, but they have been scrambled out of order. For this exercise, please time how long it takes you to solve the anagram, feeling free to stop and read on if you were unable to find the answer after three minutes or so (or less, how will anybody know).

The first anagram is:

Anagram #1:   HPUAYPN

Though certainly not simple, after a period of time it is likely that you were able to solve the anagram and came up with the word "unhappy." Let's try one more:

Anagram #2:   SPUAYPR

In general, the second anagram should have taken you longer than the first. If it didn't, that could be the intersection of your individuality with general cognitive principles or you could have been primed (chapter 5) in some way to recognize the word "papyrus" faster than "unhappy." Let's assume, however, that it did take you longer to solve Anagram #2 than #1. Why?

Both anagrams contain two Ps and one letter Y. Normally, when we encounter these three letters they form a triad at the end of words like choppy, slappy, and unhappy. Thus, because our past experiences (remember memory is a *foundational* cognitive process) have most often had those three letters going together, we are going to step by step try different combinations with those three letters together first, before we try other possibly random configurations of letters.

Papyrus, unlike unhappy, does not contain the terminal triad of -ppy, and, thus, it likely took longer because your initial problem-solving heuristics of "Y goes at the end of words" and "Two Ps go together" didn't work after you initially tried them. It took more time because you first tried the heuristic and then when that didn't work you had to employ an algorithm that entailed moving around all of the letters until they made a recognizable word.

This example should not be taken to indicate that heuristics are bad. We need heuristics for problem solving precisely because they do save resources and time. When you take your car to the mechanic because it is making an odd sound, the mechanic begins by examining what will, nine times out of ten, cause a particular sound. It is when situations don't fit with this mold that things take more time (and money).

ANALOGICAL REASONING

In some ways, the deep learning (or learning for transfer) that teachers strive for is a form of analogical reasoning. Analogies can follow the SAT format of:

knife:cut :: ruler:_____

or they can be simple forms of reasoning in which we recognize similarities between two seemingly different problems or situations. This form of reasoning can be seen in young children (Alexander et al., 1989) but isn't mature until later in life. The later maturation of this form of reasoning is likely related to the fact that, in addition to the parietal lobe, the late-maturing prefrontal cortex is likely responsible for this form of cognition (Wharton et al., 2000).

Given its reliance on the prefrontal cortex, this form of reasoning, not surprisingly, is impaired by anxiety (Tohill & Holyoak, 2000). Whether this is due to the effects of anxiety and stress upon working memory (Tohill & Holyoak, 2000) or attention (Leon & Revelle, 1985) is not currently known.

The purpose in mentioning this here is that many standardized achievement tests use analogies to try and determine a child's level of intellectual development; however, this particular type of thinking is highly susceptible to the effects of test anxiety and other emotional factors. Luckily, providing students with chances to explore and practice analogical reasoning tasks may mitigate some of the debilitating effects of anxiety upon performance (Alexander, White, Haensly, & Crimmins-Jeanes, 1987).

Unfortunately, at the end of the day, analogical reasoning in practice (rather than a:b :: c:d problems) doesn't always provide the correct answer. Just because you can use soda in cake mix doesn't mean that any liquid will suffice. Heuristics work most of the time, but not all. The key is to know *when* to stop using the heuristic and employ an algorithm instead.

Unfortunately, when time is a factor, heuristics may be unnecessarily relied upon to generate solutions, even when the answers are notably incorrect (Tsujii & Watanabe, 2010). Thus an examination of how students arrive at solutions or answers may be as important as the answer itself. Though teachers of mathematics routinely remind students to "show your work," educators in other disciplines may not. It is as important for the history teacher to understand why connections are not made as it is for the mathematics teacher to see that a student is forgetting to carry over a number.

COMMON LOGICAL MISSTEPS

Many of the problems encountered by students in a typical American classroom require deductive reasoning. Deductive reasoning relies on memory and past experiences to use general rules to draw a conclusion once information has been given about a current situation.

Valid conclusions can be drawn from scenarios provided that our premises are actually correct and the rules of logic are obeyed. The importance of accurate premises and the rules of logic can be demonstrated through the use of syllogisms. For example,

> All elementary school students are humans. (Major premise)
> All humans have brains. (Minor premise)
> Therefore, all elementary school students have brains. (Conclusion)

Both the major and minor premise from the previous example are accurate (i.e., they actually reflect what happens in the world) and the conclusion *logically* follows, thus making the reasoning valid and true. The next syllogism will demonstrate how inaccurate premises will lead to inaccurate, though *logically valid*, conclusions.

> All high school students are smart individuals.
> All smart individuals are financially wealthy.
> Therefore, all high school students are financially wealthy.

The issue with the preceding syllogism is not one of logic but of accuracy. Because at least one of the premises is flawed (the second), the conclusion that logically follows is also flawed. This is how faulty arguments persist; individuals who understand the soundness of their logical conclusions fail to consider that their premises may be inaccurate. Though beyond the scope of this current text, it is worth noting that adherence to shaky ideas following this type of reasoning is implicated in a number of social ills, including the use of stereotypes.

Equally problematic, and more germane to classrooms, is when the proper rules of logic are not followed. In particular, the use of the terms "none" or "some" introduce logical pitfalls that need to be recognized. The nouns in the following syllogism have been replaced with the letters "A," "B," and "C." The reasoning behind this will become more apparent in a moment.

> No A are B.
> No B are C.

Therefore, no A are C.

On the surface, most individuals will agree with the statement that was made. However, if we can take two accurate premises and apply them such that we still come up with an inaccurate conclusion, then it is likely due to a logical misstep. See the following two examples:

No trees are stones.	No trees are stones.
No stones are made of jelly.	No stones are alive.
Therefore, no trees are made of jelly.	Therefore, no trees are alive.

In the syllogism to the left, everything seems to make perfect (albeit silly) sense. Of course, trees are neither made of rock nor jelly, so the conclusion seems to be both logical and accurate. However, for the conclusion to be logical it must necessarily follow, meaning there aren't any other possibilities.

We can see how other possibilities can creep in when we examine the second syllogism (on the right). In this case, both premises are correct (just as they are in the previous example), except here the conclusion flies right in the face of conventional wisdom and first grade biology: trees *are* alive. The independence between trees and stones required by the first premise does not mean that any properties associated with stones then must apply to trees.

Though this may seem fairly self-evident now, Ceraso and Provitera (1971) found that adults can only identify illogical conclusions about 33 percent of the time. Remember, the conclusion of the syllogism on the left (in the previous example) is still illogical, even though it is accurate.

Although on the surface it may seem that syllogisms are somewhat removed from our everyday experiences, indeed this form of reasoning underlies much of how we arrange the world. Thus it is of paramount importance that proper rules of logic are applied and illogical arguments are recognized. Students will commonly make mistakes of this sort when terms like "none" or "some" are used.

COLLECTIVE PROBLEM SOLVING: THE GOOD, THE BAD, AND THE BLENDED

In the later 1950s, Alex Osborn put forth a series of principles that he believed would increase the number and originality of ideas that an individual comes up with: *brainstorming* in groups (1957). The term brainstorming is now relatively ubiquitous and its implementation as a pedagogical tool is pervasive, as equally likely of being found in a kindergarten classroom as in an undergraduate discussion group. However, despite the popularity and usage of the basic technique of assembling groups to find unique ways of solving problems, the cognitive psychological literature has overwhelmingly found that, in fact, brainstorming has an effect that is the *opposite* of what is desired.

In a number of studies dating back to the 1980s (Diehl & Stroebe, 1987), psychologists have examined the number and novelty of ideas that are generated by groups and by individuals. In order to make direct comparisons, actual groups are compared with *nominal* groups. For comparative purposes, if an actual group had five members working together, then a nominal group would be determined by combining the efforts of five individuals working alone.

Time and time again, evidence from both the laboratory (Diehl & Stroebe, 1987; Kohn & Smith, 2011) and the classroom (Miller, 2009) has shown that actual groups generate fewer ideas and less originality than are found when individuals work in isolation.

There are several reasons why brainstorming might stifle productivity and creativity. First, there is a diffusion of responsibility in a group setting that makes it easier for some individuals to do less or no work (social loafing), while others in the groups take the lead. Thus, though there are more members, all aren't equally pulling their weight. Though participation can be enhanced by structuring activities in such a way that grades or other indices are directly tied to the number of individual contributions to the group, such fixes have little to no effect on the originality of the ideas.

Evidence suggests that the same fixation issues that impede individual creativity are also at work in group settings (Kohn & Smith, 2011). Once an idea is recognized by the group as being a viable solution, most individual ideas that are generated afterward tend to be variations of that theme rather than being totally different.

One needs to be careful to not confuse brainstorming or its goals, as discussed here, with cooperative learning techniques. In cooperative learning, members of a group have well-defined roles that facilitate their ability to solve problems. In order to determine if the efforts of a group are successful, they are then compared against the efforts of individuals who believe that the only successful path to success is to work alone (a competitive model).

In these circumstances, there is overwhelming evidence that the learning of individuals is maximized in cooperative structures (Qin, Johnson, & Johnson, 1995). The goal and outcome of cooperative learning is just that, *learning*, and there is little doubt that learning of individuals can be optimized when effective, well-structured (and instructor-facilitated) groups are used. However, when creativity is the desired outcome of an activity, individual efforts, when conducted in a non-competitive manner (i.e., the students aren't working *against* each other), may be ideal.

When it comes to groups, there are nuances that should be considered when making decisions about whether to use cooperative learning or not. First, the nature of the problem should be considered. If the problem is one that requires multiple steps to find a solution, then a group structure is preferred. Complex problems often deplete cognitive resources and tax working memory to the point that achievement and success are impeded. Because individuals can be assigned portions of tasks while working in groups, working memory limitations can be overcome by combining individual efforts in the service of an overall solution (Kirschner, Paas, & Kirschner, 2009).

If the goal of an activity is to generate as many unique solutions as possible, perhaps to later be tested for actual practicality as usable or viable solutions, then individuals should work alone . . . at least initially. It is important that this individual brainstorming take place without competition. Then once individuals have come up with a number of solutions or answers on their own, groups with well-defined roles should be created to examine the solutions, check for errors or inaccuracies, and think about implementation.

This blended approach to problem solving thus (1) minimizes creative fixation that may occur with groups and (2) utilizes a collective working memory that can work through the cognitive limitations of individuals.

OVERCOMING BARRIERS TO CREATIVITY

Creativity is a form of divergent thinking that results in the development of something that is novel. Classical theories maintain that there are four stages of creative thinking: preparation, incubation, illumination, and verification (Lubart, 2001; Torrance, 1974). The preparation stage is used to prepare the mind by considering all aspects of the problem. The incubation period was believed to then be necessary for "offline" processing (i.e., indirect thinking) to take place that would then lead to the "Eureka!" moment when the solution to the problem was found (illumination).

Incubation was seen as a "break" from actively thinking about the problem. Finally, a verification of the utility and/or novelty of the creative output is needed. Though these stages appeal to our sense of creative works "springing" into an artist's or scientist's mind from some otherworldly muse, modern theories of creativity suggest they may not be needed (Lubart, 2001).

There is now evidence that suggests that the incubation stage, which was once seen as being necessary to release the mind from proactive interference, may not be necessary for creative thought. Some studies have shown that focused attention—and not rest—is the key to some forms of creativity (e.g., De Dreu et al., 2012).

One problem with examining creativity in people is the fact that many feel that it is too subjective to measure. Psychologists, however, have developed four general criteria that they use to gauge whether someone is creative: fluency, flexibility, originality, and elaboration (Torrance, 1974). As can be seen from this list, there is more to being a creative thinker than merely being original.

But what about creativity in the classroom? Are there ways to help or hinder divergent thinking? My students love examples. Whenever I have major projects, papers, or other summative assessments that are due at the end of a semester, prototypes are requested. Though it may seem counterintuitive, I only provide exemplars (usually stellar papers from past students) for the most straightforward of assessments: research papers.

For example, in a graduate-level class on early language development, my students are required to create a children's book that utilizes cognitive principles learned in the class (sound familiar?) and make it accessible to children for whom English is a second language (they are allowed to tailor the book based on the hypothetical child's first language, e.g., Spanish). Without an example of what the book is "supposed to look like," my students must rely on their own intuition, their interpretation of the formatting rules, and their own ideas related to what a children's book does or *should* look like.

The reason that I don't provide sample books for my students is that I don't want to stifle their creativity. The assessment is designed so that the students have the opportunity to integrate the principles that I've taught them using what they know from their own professional experience—just as I want them to do in their own classrooms. By providing them with an example, I am showing them exactly what *they* think I want and am erecting unnecessary boundaries that may restrict their creative process.

Indeed, research has shown that examples constrain creativity. Undergraduate students were given 20 minutes to draw as many toys or aliens as they could. Half of the students (for both toys and aliens) were shown examples of what novel aliens or toys would look like 90 seconds before they drew and half of the students weren't shown anything.

Blind (i.e., the analyst didn't know whether the participant had seen the example or not) analysis of the number of novel features showed a robust *conformity effect*: those individuals who saw the examples incorporated many more of those features into their drawings than the students who weren't given examples. This effect persisted even with a delay (about 20 minutes) introduced between the presentation of the examples and the drawing task.

Adherence to the examples was seen even when students were explicitly told that they should move beyond the features depicted in the examples (Smith, Ward, & Schumacher, 1993). These findings reinforce the notion that examples create a form of *fixation*, whereby it is difficult for the mind to come up with ideas other than those that were shown. The take-home message is clear: if creative thinking is desired, avoid using examples.

In addition to the type of fixedness just discussed, individuals can also fail to think about objects in novel ways. *Functional fixedness* occurs when our perception of an object is bound by how it is normally used (Duncker, 1945; Maier, 1931). In the classic demonstration, participants were given a box of thumbtacks, a candle, and a book of matches and were told to attach the candle to the wall so that it wouldn't drip on the floor. Though most of the participants attempted to directly tack the candle to the wall or in some way use melted wax to adhere the candle, a few thought "outside of the box" . . . literally. Those individuals used the thumbtacks to attach the box to the wall and set the candle in the box. For most participants, the inability to see the box as anything but a container was a block to its creative use.

One way to overcome functional fixedness is to utilize what is called a *generic parts technique* (GPT). To use the GPT, one considers all of the aspects and properties of an item, even those that might seem somewhat obscure. So for example, when thinking of a candle, a seemingly obscure property (that at least may not immediately come to mind) is the fact that a string (i.e., the wick) runs through most of the length of a candle. When approached in this way, a candle may actually be used to tie things together (McCaffery, 2012). Although successful implementation of this technique in classroom settings has not yet been demonstrated, it may prove fruitful in learning situations in which divergent thinking is the desired outcome.

POINTS TO REMEMBER

- Directed thinking is related to convergent thought, whereby experience is used to solve a problem. Creativity is akin to divergent thought which may lead to novel solutions.
- Well-defined problems have initial states, goal states, and operators that are all known.
- The connectivity of the brain may be the neurological substrate of creativity.
- Algorithms and heuristics are used to problem solve.
- Heuristics work most of the time; however, stress, anxiety, and time constraints may affect awareness of the success of using a particular strategy.
- Examining *how* students arrive at solutions may be as important as *knowing* whether they were correct.

- Logical inaccuracies can occur when students incorrectly solve syllogisms, particularly those that include statements about "some" or "none."
- Group brainstorming actually inhibits creativity. Individuals generate more novel solutions to problems when they brainstorm alone.
- Some creative endeavors, such as music, may benefit from focused attention.
- Providing examples may contextually constrain the creativity of students.
- A generic parts technique may be useful for helping students overcome functional fixedness.

REFERENCES

Alexander, P. A., White, C. S., Haensly, P. A., & Crimmins-Jeanes, M. (1987). Training in analogical reasoning. *American Educational Research Journal, 24*(3), 387–404.

Alexander, P. A., Willson, V. L., White, C. S., Fuqua, J. D., Clark, G. D., Wilson, A. F., & Kulikowich, J. M. (1989). Development of analogical reasoning in 4- and 5-year-old children. *Cognitive Development, 4*(1), 65–88.

Ceraso, J., & Provitera, A. (1971). Sources of error in syllogistic reasoning. *Cognitive Psychology, 2*(4), 400–410.

De Dreu, C. K., Nijstad, B. A., Baas, M., Wolsink, I., & Roskes, M. (2012). Working memory benefits creative insight, musical improvisation, and original ideation through maintained task-focused attention. *Personality and Social Psychology Bulletin, 38*(5), 656–669.

Diehl, M., & Stroebe, W. (1987). Productivity loss in brainstorming groups: Toward the solution of a riddle. *Journal of Personality and Social Psychology, 53*(3), 497–509.

Dietrich, A., & Kanso, R. (2010). A review of EEG, ERP, and neuroimaging studies of creativity and insight. *Psychological Bulletin, 136*, 822–848.

Duncker, K. (1945). On problem solving. *Psychological Monographs, 58*, 113.

Goel, V., Buchel, C., Frith, C., & Dolan, R. J. (2000). Dissociation of mechanisms underlying syllogistic reasoning. *NeuroImage, 12* (5), 504–514.

Goel, V., & Dolan, R. J. (2003). Explaining modulation of reasoning by belief. *Cognition, 87*, B11–B22.

Guilford, J. P. (1967). *The nature of human intelligence*. New York: McGraw-Hill Companies.

Heilman, K. M., Nadeau, S. E., & Beversdorf, D. O. (2003). Creative innovation: Possible brain mechanisms. *Neurocase, 9*, 369–379.

Jausovec, N., & Jausovec, K. (2000). EEG activity during the performance of complex mental problems. *International Journal of Psychophysiology, 36*, 73–88.

Kirschner, F., Paas, F., & Kirschner, P. A. (2009). A cognitive load approach to collaborative learning: United brains for complex tasks. *Educational Psychology Review, 21*, 31–42.

Kohn, N. W., & Smith, S. M. (2011). Collaborative fixation: Effects of others' ideas on brainstorming. *Applied Cognitive Psychology, 25*(3), 359–371.

Leon, M. R., & Revelle, W. (1985). Effects of anxiety on analogical reasoning: A test of three theoretical models. *Journal of Personality and Social Psychology, 49*(5), 1302.

Lubart, T. I. (2001). Models of the creative process: Past, present and future. *Creativity Research Journal, 13*(3–4), 295–308.

Maier, N. R. F. (1931). Reasoning in humans: II. The solution of a problem and its appearance in consciousness. *Comparative Psychology, 12*, 181–194.

McCaffrey, T. (2012). Innovation relies on the obscure: A key to overcoming the classic problem of functional fixedness. *Psychological Science, 23*(3), 215–218.

Miller, L. (2009). Evidence-based instruction: A classroom experiment comparing nominal and brainstorming groups. *Organization Management Journal, 6,* 229–238.

Moore, D. W., Bhadelia, R. A., Billings, R. L., Fulwiler, C., Heilman, K. M., Rood, K. M. J., & Gansler, D. A. (2009). Hemispheric connectivity and the visual-spatial divergent-thinking component of creativity. *Brain and Cognition, 70,* 267–272.

Osborn, A. (1957). *Applied imagination.* New York: Scribner.

Qin, Z., Johnson, D. W., & Johnson, R. T. (1995). Cooperative versus competitive efforts and problem solving. *Review of Educational Research, 65,* 129–143.

Smith, S. M., Ward, T. B., & Schumacher, J. S. (1993). Constraining effects of examples in a creative generation task. *Memory & Cognition, 21*(6), 837–845.

Slavin, R. E. (1983). When does cooperative learning increase student achievement? *Psychological Bulletin, 94*(3), 429–445.

Takeuchi, H., Taki, Y., Sassa, Y., Hashizume, H., Sekiguchi, A., Fukushima, A., & Kawashima, R. (2010). White matter structures associated with creativity: Evidence from diffusion tensor imaging. *Neuroimage, 51,* 11–18.

Takeuchi, H., Taki, Y., Hashizume, H., Sassa, Y., Nagase, T., Nouchi, R., & Kawashima, R. (2012). The association between resting functional connectivity and creativity. *Cerebral Cortex, 22*(12>, 2921-2929.

Tohill, J. M., & Holyoak, K. J. (2000). The impact of anxiety on analogical reasoning. *Thinking & Reasoning, 6*(1), 27–40.

Torrance, E.P. (1974). *The Torrance Tests of Creative Thinking: Norms-Technical Manual.* Lexington, MA: Personnel Press.

Tsujii, T., & Watanabe, S. (2010). Neural correlates of belief-bias reasoning under time pressure: a near-infrared spectrosopy study. *Neuroimage, 50*(3), 1320-1326.

Wharton, C. M., Grafman, J., Flitman, S. S., Hansen, E. K., Brauner, J., Marks, A., & Honda, M. (2000). Toward neuroanatomical models of analogy: A positron emission tomography study of analogical mapping. *Cognitive Psychology, 40*(3), 173–197.

Witelson, S. F. (1985). The brain connection: The corpus callosum is larger in lefthanders. *Science, 229,* 665–668.

TEN
Synthesis

CODA

Originally, I wanted to write a series of articles for educators that would effectively merge research on cognition and the brain with education to enhance curriculum and instruction. Indeed, one of those articles, *Taking on Multitasking* (2011), is the basis for some of the strategies mentioned in chapter 3 on attention. That article was well received; however, the amount of attention paid to articles in professional magazines is somewhat ephemeral.

My own research, conducted with Dr. Naomi Schoenfeld, showed that books and not articles were the primary source that teachers used for information about so-called brain-based strategies (Rekart, Schoenfeld, Himmelberger, & Pelletier, 2012). Taken together, these two pieces of information suggested to me that if I were going to truly make a difference and further the cause of integrating cognitive and neuroscientific research into education, that I needed a new plan. So, I changed course and decided to write a book—this book—*about* articles.

Though some well-written books for educators are actually based in the research literature, there are others, many of which are quite popular, that offer little more than the unsubstantiated claims of the author(s). Being able to differentiate between the former and the latter can be difficult. Though it is impossible to completely remove one's bias from any endeavor, I have strived to ensure that this text is one that refrains, whenever possible, from conjecture.

My intent was to bring cognitive psychology and brain science out of the hygienic but isolated confines of the laboratory and into the everyday noisiness of the classroom. Too often, professional practice and academe occupy separate silos. What is needed is for the two to mutually complement and expand the other. I hope I have brought to light what it means for information to flow from the university to the schools. The opposite direction is more problematic but no less important. Bidirectional communication can only exist if both sides are willing to listen to each other and if both are destinations for information. The center won't hold if one side is always the transmitter and the other the receiver.

BARRIERS AND SOLUTIONS TO IMPLEMENTING RESEARCH FINDINGS IN THE CLASSROOM

One of my favorite classes to teach is a graduate education course on the fundamentals of research. This course, which is ED-501 (all Master's-level courses are 500- and 600-level), should be one of the first few taken as students work toward Master's degrees and CAGS; however, it is most often the last. There are many reasons why students delay the course, including greater interest in other classes, intimidation by the subject matter, and scheduling conflicts. However, the one reason that is the most problematic is that many students don't believe that the class will be of any use to them.

To explore this last rationale further, we must first examine who the students I am writing about are. My students are primarily educators, many of whom have years of classroom experience. Many of these students are not actually pursuing their first Master's, but in some cases a second (or third) or are trying to fulfill the requirements for a post-baccalaureate certificate program. These students are focused on learning about the concepts which they believe will directly impact their practice. Their interest is in special education, reading, autism, or emotional and behavioral difficulties—not research. Thus it is my job to not only teach them the fundamentals of research design and theory but to convince them of the utility of research in their own professional practice.

Indeed, a common sentiment that has been echoed over the years that I've taught the class is "Research doesn't apply to education." When I ask exactly why research isn't applicable, I am told that *everybody* learns *differently*. This last piece, which is the basis for a widespread dismissal of research, is only half correct.

What is the common admonition from a teacher the night before an examination? "Be sure to study . . ." is the advice that the educator gives to the class. Are loud noises allowed during an examination? Are students allowed to chew gum and consequently pop bubbles loudly, chat about non-test-related subjects, or hum their favorite tunes out loud? Of course, the answer to all of these questions is a resounding "No." And the reason why teachers recommend studying before an examination and require silence during testing is because they believe that *in general* students need to review material and have an absence of distractions to do well on an exam. It is the absolute amount of studying and the degree of quiet that vary from child to child.

Our modern notions of learning styles have made great contributions to the classroom, both in terms of student success and teacher involvement. However, we have to remember that a teacher doesn't lecture 20 different ways to reach 20 different students simultaneously. Unfortunately, the focus over the past quarter-century or so on differentiated instruction has left most teachers with the notion that somehow general theories of learning, which are firmly rooted in research, are not applicable to education. It is these very same general principles of pedagogy, however, that are the foundation upon which education stands. Even the best, most successful (in terms of student success) teachers stand in front of a classroom and deliver information to 20 or more students in one way. What contributes to these teachers' success is that they are able to simultaneously reach most of their class because of the manner in which they deliver the information, concepts, and strategies to be learned. By using best practices regarding *collectivistic* instruction, the teacher is then able to focus upon the few students for whom the first go-round didn't click.

Once the premise that research about general learning principles is not of use to education is rejected, there are still other barriers that remain. As a member of the Association for Psychological Science (APS), which is a professional organization comprised of individuals for whom psychological research (not therapy) is their primary interest, I subscribe to four different scientific journals.

These journals, which are among the most respected in all of psychology, are delivered to my office every month. The day that one of them, *Psychological Science*, arrives (i.e., Journal Day) is . . . and I know how this sounds . . . *magical*. For me (yes, I'm *that* guy), it is Christmas morning. It feels good to know what current research in all areas of psychology is telling us about the human brain and behavior. I don't know what new techniques or elegant designs await me when I open up the cover. It is exciting to be in touch with the new interpretations of old theories and the testing of intriguing new hypotheses. It feels good to be on the cutting edge. Plus, I love new journal smell.

I am not alone in my joyful glee when Journal Day arrives. I am willing to wager that the clapping and dancing (at least that is what I'm doing in my mind; it isn't dignified to actually do so on campus) that accompany Journal Day takes place many times over in academic settings across this country, if not the world. Academics live for this stuff and this exuberance over research can be channeled to assist educators with their own practice.

Professional learning communities (PLCs) were designed as a way to allow professionals to discuss topics of interest that would support their own career development in an interactive and collaborative manner. One key component to PLCs is that they are driven and directed by the members; thus there is an ownership of the topics and the growth that takes place. However, what has not, to my knowledge, become widespread is the expansion of PLCs to routinely include outside experts. Certainly experts are brought in through the books that often play a central role in PLCs; however, this is not the same as having a flesh-and-blood individual with whom to collaborate.

I have recommended (2012) that academics be asked to join PLCs in an advisory role. The academics in these *integrated* PLCs (iPLCs) would then gather pertinent research articles and evidence to actually answer any questions or topics that the educators within the iPLC would decide to cover. Then working together, the academic can help decipher, if necessary, statistical jargon, research designs, and so forth to facilitate critical readings of the research.

Although the knowledge is supplied by the academic, the interpretation of the articles and their ramifications for practice would be the result of the discussions and input of the faculty iPLC members. Relationships such as these could then ripple out into further endeavors, perhaps those that could facilitate projects in which the college or university professor(s) and K–12 faculty work together as co-equal partners by designing and researching the implementation of strategies that have the research literature as their basis.

Such collaborations could then potentially increase the number of educators who coauthor research on classroom teaching and learning (Schoenfeld, Towson, & Rekart, in review). An additional advantage of working with academics is that they have access to journals that many teachers do not. I've listed (in the following) the titles of journals that often contain articles that are of direct relevance to educators. Indeed, if you look through the bibliographies for each of the chapters, you'll find the majority of papers came from many of these journals.

Respected, Peer-Reviewed Journals of Relevance for Educators

(*journals with review articles)

American Educational Research Journal
British Journal of Educational Psychology
Cognition
Cognition & Emotion
Educational Researcher
Emotion
Journal of Emotional and Behavioral Disorders
Journal of Educational Research
Journal of Experimental Psychology: Learning, Memory, and Cognition
Journal of Personality and Social Psychology

Learning & Memory
Memory
*Mind, Brain, and Education**
Nature
*Nature Reviews Neuroscience**
*Perspectives in Psychological Science**
Proceedings of the National Academy of Sciences, U.S.A. (PNAS)
Psychological Science
*Psychological Science in the Public Interest**
Science
*Trends in Cognitive Sciences**
*Trends in Neurosciences**

For those educators who wish to stay informed of new advances, there are a number of ways to do this, even without institutional support. First, over the last ten years there has been a proliferation of what are called "open-access" journals. Rather than being primarily supported through subscriptions from college and university libraries, these publications are largely made possible through corporate endowments or the support of professional organizations. Some charge a small administrative fee to the authors of accepted manuscripts. All of the ones listed below are peer reviewed.

Contemporary Issues in Technology and Teacher Education
Creative Education
Current Issues in Comparative Education
Current Issues in Education
Early Childhood Research & Practice
Education Next
Education Research International
Interdisciplinary Journal of Problem-based Learning
International Electronic Journal of Health Education
International Journal for Mathematics Teaching and Learning
International Journal of Education
International Journal of Education Policy and Leadership
Journal of Educators Online
Journal of Scholarship and Practice
Practical Assessment, Research & Evaluation
Research in Middle Level Education Online
The New Educator
The School Community Journal

In addition, there are a number of good sites on the internet where solid, research-based evidence may be found. The Institute of Education Sciences (IES) is the branch of the federal Department of Education that is responsible for providing and disseminating empirical evidence in support of policies and strategies for curriculum, instruction, and assessment. The homepage for this non-partisan center is:

http://ies.ed.gov/

In addition, a visit to the What Works Clearinghouse, which is administered through the IES, can provide quick summaries of research, including whether the methodologies employed by the authors are rigorous enough to be used as the basis for practice. The What Works Clearinghouse may be found at:

http://ies.ed.gov/ncee/wwc/

Thus there are numerous ways for educators to stay abreast of current findings in cognitive psychology and neuroscience that may be of relevance.

THE FUTURE OF E-LEARNING

In previous chapters, we discussed possible issues with alternative and supplementary educational paradigms, like the Khan Academy, baby media, and even the Mozart (lack of an) effect. What is so alluring about these types of programs is their deceptive ease. We want to believe that deep and lasting learning will take place by merely watching a video. A major problem with many of these initiatives, however, is that they work against millions of years of evolution.

We are social animals and our brains evolved elaborate and reliable mechanisms to facilitate social interactions. Being social animals, our learning is facilitated by interacting with others. Through the use of gestures or by making eye contact, we let our brains know that, in fact, we are interacting, which in turn activates regions necessary for learning. Where is the eye contact when we watch pre-recorded videos?

What takes place in a classroom *matters*. Teachers *matter*. A teacher, unlike a video, knows her students. Knows when a student understands something or doesn't. A teacher isn't rewound only to repeat herself with the exact same explanation presented using the exact same words. No. The best teachers present information using different perspectives, tailoring their instruction for the students for whom some challenges may be present. This book is written with teachers in mind. The strategies and techniques discussed do not require any additional fees. How specifically these strategies should be implemented is up to you. You know your class and your students better than anyone. Use your professional expertise and judgment to see what works for you and what doesn't.

REVISITING INTELLIGENCE

Finally, I want to end this book by briefly tackling a touchy subject. The term *intelligence* can evoke many different feelings. For many educators, it represents a concept that they must work against; perhaps by trying to convince parents that their child's talents and potential are not reducible to a single number or set of scores. Part of the problem with something as potentially large as intelligence is how abstract it is. Height can be readily measured, seen, and compared; it is concrete. What's more, it exists independently of context; Judy is the same height regardless of if she is in Akron or Nashua. Intelligence, however, is abstract. There is little to no agreement about *what* intelligence is, let alone how to measure it (or if it even can be measured).

Though of all the theories of intelligence that have been floated through the years, my personal favorite is that of Perkins (1995) because of the importance he gives to the brain and its wiring. I could go on and on about the pros and cons of his and many other theories; however, there is no need. This book, in essence, was about intelligence. All of the cognitive processes that we've discussed are related to an individual's ability to function within the world. Rather than focus on what intelligence *is* or how best to measure it, I think time is better spent by working to facilitate each of its components.

In the end, it is best to think of changes that can be made through instruction. To this end, the important relationship between good pedagogy, the rewiring of the brain (plasticity), and student demonstrations of learning (performance) are critical.

REFERENCES

Rekart, J. L. (2011). Taking on multitasking. *Phi Delta Kappan*, 93(4), 60-63.
Rekart, J. L. (2012). Meeting of the minds. *Principal*, 91(5), 45-46.
Rekart, J. L., Schoenfeld, N., Himmelberger, Z., & Pelletier, C. (2012). Assessing K–12 educator and college student beliefs and knowledge about the brain. Association for Psychological Science, Chicago, IL, II–49.
Perkins, D. (1995). Outsmarting IQ: The emerging science of learnable intelligence. New York: Simon & Schuster.
Schoenfeld, N., Towson, D., & Rekart, J. L. (2013). Who is writing? *Behavioral Disorders*, in press.